FIFTEENTH CENTURY: THE PROSPECT OF EUROPE

THE FIFTEENTH CENTURY: THE PROSPECT OF EUROPE

MARGARET ASTON

with 153 illustrations, 24 in colour

THAMES AND HUDSON

To E.E.B. and K.D.B.

© 1968 Thames and Hudson Ltd, London

Reprinted 1994

ISBN 0-500-33009-3

Printed and bound in Singapore by C.S. Graphics

CONTENTS

'*I look upon a picture with no less pleasure . . . than I read a good history. They both indeed are pictures, only the historian paints with words, and the painter with his pencil.*'
L. B. ALBERTI, *De Re Aedificatoria*

FOREWORD

This book owes much to many. Experts will recognize its debts; I would like others to discover them. It is impossible to write on such a subject without being heavily indebted and, since my plunderings are recorded only indirectly and partially in the bibliography, I can only hope that I have not been guilty of too many injustices.

I am very grateful to all those who have spent time on the book and have given me help and advice. Professor R. W. Southern read it in typescript and made many valuable and penetrating criticisms. I have also benefited greatly from the comments and suggestions of Professor G. Barraclough, Mrs B. M. Jones and Dr J. W. Stoye. Mr Elliott Nixon has kindly helped me with the proofs. If I have failed at every point to take the advice which has been offered I hope to be forgiven; it has not been for lack of consideration. At various stages, through conversation, correspondence, and presents of articles and books, my work has been helped and encouraged by the generosity of Professor F. M. Bartoš of Prague. I also wish to thank Professor Hans Baron and Dr Gordon Leff for having kindly allowed me to read copies of their work in advance of publication. And I am indebted to Professor E. H. Gombrich for a conversation which directed my attention to various matters. For help with the illustrations thanks are due to Miss Emily Lane, and, for his patience and assistance as editor, a special debt belongs to Mr Stanley Baron.

It is a pleasure to return thanks to the Trustees of Amherst College for the opportunity to work in the Folger Shakespeare Library, whose courteous staff and excellent resources have eased the completion of the book. Other libraries for whose good services I am grateful are the University Library, Cambridge, The British Museum, and the Library of Congress, Washington, D.C.

Finally I thank the Principal and Fellows of Newnham College, Cambridge, who, by electing me to the Jenner Research Fellowship for the year 1965–66 granted me, among other benefits, freedom as Virginia Woolf defined it to the college Arts Society in 1928 – 'five hundred a year and a room with a lock on the door'.

The Folger Shakespeare Library,
Washington, D.C.   *30 March 1967*

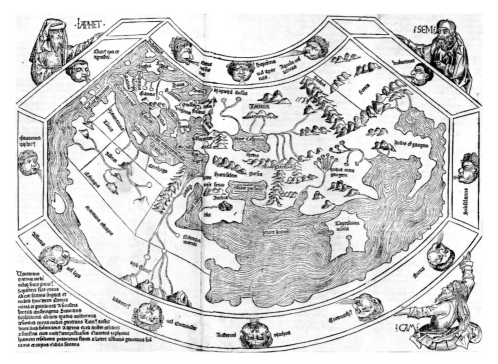

1 The fall of Trebizond in 1461.
This detail from
a Florentine cassone
was painted about 1475

2 The world of fifteenth-century
cartographic convention with Jerusalem
at the centre and
a land-locked Indian Ocean

The remotest of the kings has been deafened by the sound of the ocean waves . . . he does not hear our sighs but being buried in the extreme West has no care for what the East is doing. PETRARCH, *Life of Solitude* (1346)

Jesus! said I, is there here a new world? Sure, said he, it is never a jot new, but it is commonly reported, that, without this, there is an earth, whereof the inhabitants enjoy the light of a sun and moon, and that it is full of, and replenished with, very good commodities; but yet this is more ancient than that.
RABELAIS, *Pantagruel* (1532)

In 1500 Europe existed. For the world of a century or so earlier such a proposition is altogether more doubtful. In the latter part of the fourteenth century Christendom was more meaningful than Europe, and the horizons of the Christian world were steadily contracting under the pressure of Turkish expansion in the east. By 1500 the Portuguese were already harvesting the profits of their first seaborne expedition to India and Columbus had returned to Castile from his third voyage of exploration to the west. Christian Europe stood poised between a new balance of east and west, and different European perspectives emerged as the quadripartite world of four continents came to replace the time-honoured triplicate world, divisible among the sons of Noah. In the fifteenth century Christendom was giving way to Europe; it became possible to be 'European'.

Few contemporaries could see these changes. Between Petrarch and Rabelais, from Marsilio of Padua to Leonardo da Vinci, the number of those whose comprehension of their times can be called European certainly increased, but was always limited. As Petrarch himself pointed out, the learned are always few, and in recovering the past it is important to remember the limitations of contemporary knowledge which are themselves a part of history. The fifteenth

9

century revolutionized both the numbers of learners and the opportunities for learning, but it was long before the full impact of the most momentous discoveries of the time became evident. America had to be discovered at least twice – once by Columbus and again by Amérigo Vespucci. If knowledge, even of contemporary events, was hard to come by at the time, understanding is always a different sort of gift, and things are by no means always recognized for what they are at the moment when they acquire a name. Even for those best placed to know the facts of geographical discovery (which now seem such salient features of the period), there were other transformations which in their age seemed more important. Fifteenth-century Europe was reoriented internally as well as externally and to contemporaries the inner transformations were by far the more significant.

Those whose lives spanned the latter part of the fourteenth century and the beginning of the fifteenth were conscious of living in a period of disaster. Life and faith seemed to be endangered by a double threat: one was the expansion of Islam in the shape of the Ottoman Turks; the other was a disease, the plague. The sense of the encroaching east, which had already eaten away so much of eastern Christendom before the fifteenth century, impressed contemporaries – in ways which our generation is well-fitted to understand – with the feeling that their world was a world in decline. The forces of expansion seemed to belong to the east while the west was subjected to decay. Politicians and moralizers, as always connecting public calamity with private improvement, placed the Turk near the centre of every argument.

Four years before the end of the fourteenth century a great crusading force, drawn from all the major kingdoms of the west, suffered a devastating defeat at the hands of the Sultan Bajezid I, on the heights above the Danube at Nicopolis. The distinguished leaders who were taken captive included the heir of the duke of Burgundy, two cousins of the French king, and the marshal of France. So incredible was the scale of the disaster that the first survivors who straggled home to France were imprisoned on account of their reports. In the years that followed, the west had to pay for its failure not only in crippling ransoms for the leaders who had been taken, but also in its own deteriorating position in the east. 'Believe me,' cautioned Coluccio Salutati, chancellor of Florence (1375–1406), writing in 1397 to one of the princes attending the diet which was meeting at Frankfurt, 'unless God intervenes and unless you and others take proper precautions, these people will achieve greater successes than you think.' For once the alarmists of the day were justified. Nicopolis was far from ending the era of crusading hopes and preparations, but in the century that followed, talk about such matters enormously exceeded action, and the area of land in Christian hands continued to be narrowed in the east.

3 The advance of the Turks into Europe, which began with the conquest of Gallipoli in 1354, continued through and well beyond the fifteenth century. The reign of Mohammed II (1451–81) was a time of particularly rapid expansion

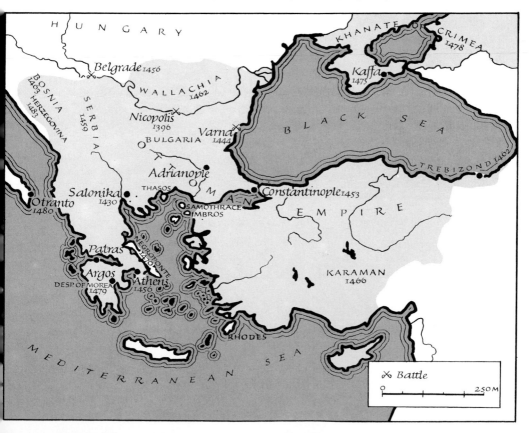

In 1430 Salonika, which the Venetians had acquired seven years earlier, fell with much bloodshed and caused new waves of horror in Europe. In 1444 the story of Nicopolis was repeated at Varna on the Black Sea, wrecking what had been high hopes of a combined Hungarian-Polish drive against the Turks. In the 1450s Serbia was overrun; Constantinople and Athens fell; the Aegean islands of Imbros, Thasos and Samothrace were taken. In the 1460s went Bosnia, and the last outposts of the Greek empire of Trebizond on

NAVE·DEL·ARMER

4, 5 After the great Turkish victory at Nicopolis in 1396, the duke of Burgundy had to pay a vast ransom (below) for the captured leaders, including his son, the Count of Nevers. At the end of the fifteenth century the Battle of Zonchio (left) established Turkish power at sea

the Black Sea and of the Greek Despotate of the Paleologi in the Morea (the Peloponnese). 'The Turks are devastating one country after another,' lamented Pope Pius II in 1463, and this same year the Venetians, having lost their colony at Argos, opened hostilities against the conquering Mohammed II which culminated in 1470 in their loss of Negroponte (Euboea) – an event more serious for Venice than the earlier fall of Constantinople. By the end of the 1470s the Turks were masters of the Black Sea and of the northern Aegean; it

13

even appeared that they might gain control over the Adriatic. The fears for Italy which were causing anxiety in Toulouse and even in England seemed to have been realized when Mohammed in the last year of his life gained a temporary foothold on Italian soil at Otranto in 1480. Rome itself seemed to be threatened. 'So strong the Turks have grown to be,' wrote Sebastian Brant (1458–1521) in the 1490s, driving home the lesson with a full list of their conquests, 'They hold the ocean not alone,/The Danube too is now their own.' They had attacked Apulia, tomorrow it would be the turn of Italy; the four patriarchates of the east had all been lost to them, might not Rome be the next victim?

The fall of Constantinople in 1453 became significant as a dramatic, symbolic episode in a long series of events. It was an objective of Turkish policy long before it became the obsession of Mohammed II. Constantinople was besieged at the opening of the fifteenth century; it was blockaded again in 1422; as early as 1390 the calculating Venetian authorities were issuing instructions to one of their embassies which allowed for the city's being found in Turkish hands.

6, 7 Mohammed II (above) was 19 when he became sultan in 1451, and had already determined to conquer Constantinople (right, in 1420)

The survival of the Greek capital until the middle of the century is in some ways more surprising than its ultimate fall, so long foreseeable, so long in coming. Mohammed's conquest came to be seen as a catastrophic landmark because it was a representative event. It stood both for rising humanist hopes and for a long accumulation of guilt and fear. Rulers and politicians for more than a century before and after 1453 lived with anxiety about the challenging problems of the east. And preachers, pounding away in the wake of politicians, used the Turk to drive home moral truths. 'Do you think the Turk will come into Italy this year?' asked one of the characters in Machiavelli's *Mandragola*, which was set in the Florence of 1504. 'Yes,' answered Fra Timoteo, 'if you do not say your prayers.' Machiavelli's comedy was in Boccaccio's tradition, and the laugh was still on the churchman. Although fears of the Turk continued to be real and applicable to others besides ecclesiastics and statesmen, the moralists who went on reiterating old arguments in a world which was changing began to sound, as they usually do, a generation out of date.

The shadow of the plague, like the fear of the Turk, lay across the whole century. After the first devastating pandemic of 1347–50 had spread through all the countries of western Europe, reducing the population in many areas by as much as a third or a half, the 'Black Death' (as it was later called) became established in the west. As time went on, general outbreaks gave way to regional and local attacks of varying duration and mortality, but plague remained a constant visible phenomenon. From the time of Boccaccio and Orcagna down to that of Erasmus and Dürer and beyond, the actions and observations of writers and painters – as well as of others – reflect the effects of the disease.

> There will not be enough men left to bury the dead; nor means to dig enough graves. So many will lie dead in the houses, that men will go through the streets crying, 'send forth your dead!' And the dead will be heaped in carts and on horses; they will be piled up and burnt. Men will pass through the streets crying aloud, 'Are there any dead? Are there any dead?'

8–10 Representations of mortality.

Left, Death taking the printers and book-seller (the earliest known depiction, 1499, of a printer's office). Below, the triumph of death, an illustration of 1470–80, in which the foremost buffalo drawing the cart on which Death stands, is shown treading on the body of a priest and the head and crown of a king

In the illustration on the right from an early fifteenth-century Book of Hours, the dead man lies naked as all must leave the world, before the Lord. Overhead St Michael attacks the devil for possession of the soul of the deceased ▶

Savonarola's apocalyptic message was still vivid to the Florentines to whom he preached it in 1496, as it had been to their predecessors five generations earlier when Boccaccio had removed his group of imaginary story-tellers from the horrors of the city to the self-contained delights of their country retreat. The impact of the plague was unprecedented and its impression ineffaceable, even to those who were accustomed to a high annual mortality as a normal state of affairs. Would posterity ever believe it, Petrarch wondered, when the sight of so many corpses, vacant houses, deserted towns and neglected countryside, seemed dreamlike even to those who witnessed them? The later Middle Ages was a period which, not unlike our own, had been made aware of death on a hitherto inconceivable scale. It was an experience which was conducive to self-examination, to the appraisal of accepted values. 'How can it even be called a life', asked Thomas à Kempis, 'which begets so many deaths and plagues?' The fifteenth century, like the fourteenth, exemplified the perennial dichotomy of human nature responding to that question – Stoic and Epicurean. If there were numerous successors to the escapists portrayed in the *Decameron*, there were many others who followed the example of Petrarch's Carthusian brother Gherardo, who refused to leave his monastery on his prior's advice in 1348, and survived to bury all the thirty monks who remained with him.

By the end of the fifteenth century plague mortality had left its mark in many places – in art and literature and in life. People had learnt to live with as well as to flee from the pestilence. The endemic nature of the disease led to medical and religious counter-measures. Milan and Bologna, for instance, devised systems of health certificates and quarantine to try to ensure that travellers did not bring plague from other areas. Special saints, like St Sebastian and St Roch

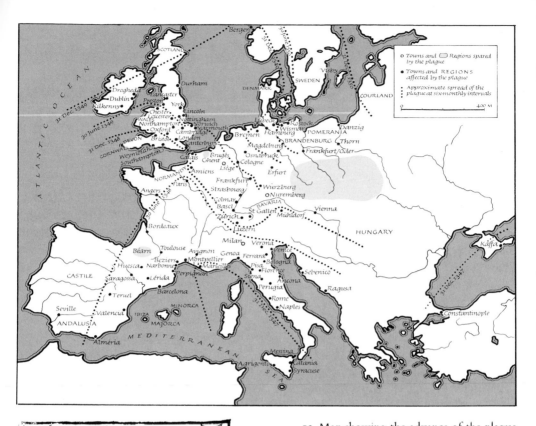

12 Map showing the advance of the plague
as it spread across Europe
from the east in 1347–50

11, 13 Processions of flagellants (opposite),
with scourges and distinctive robes,
increased with the plague and were banned
by the papacy in 1349.
St Sebastian (left) was invoked
for protection against 'plague,
languishing sickness, sudden death
and all unusual deaths'

19

(appropriated by the Venetians) were cultivated as particular defenders against the disease. Venice was specially vulnerable to plague because of her commercial links with the east, and the city elaborated a procedure for inspecting incoming goods and persons on an island set aside for that purpose. As in many other spheres, a great deal of effort was devoted to a hopeless cause. The plague could not be arrested and continued to recur, particularly in densely populated places. The ecclesiastical councils of Constance, Basel and Ferrara–Florence, the Bohemian assembly at Prague in 1450 and the jubilee at Rome in the same year were all visited by outbreaks. There were fourteen years of epidemic in Spain between 1391 and 1457, Perugia in the course of the fifteenth century had eight attacks affecting nineteen years, and many towns such as Hamburg, Nuremberg and Cologne suffered ten or more epidemics. Obits in the later Middle Ages were remembered more often than birthdays. Artists celebrated mortality by the triumph of death south of the Alps and by the dance of death in the north. *Inter mortuos mortem exspectans* could have served as the motto for a number of creative individuals of the century.

The visible remains of the fifteenth century (as of most ages) bear witness more to its prosperity than to its adversity. At the time, depopulation long continued to be evident. And although some cities were growing steadily, and economic recovery (beginning perhaps about 1470 in France and England) may have become general in the later years of the century, it is doubtful whether the population of Europe as a whole regained its pre-plague level until well into the sixteenth century. While to us the whole world of the Middle Ages naturally seems very underpopulated, one effect of the plague was to make contemporaries unusually sensitive to questions of demography, conscious of the prosperity which lay in numbers. The contrasts between different regions were certainly striking. In certain areas of Germany the decline of population left as much as 50 to 60 per cent of once cultivated land unoccupied. The kingdoms of the Iberian peninsula (which likewise failed to recuperate until a later period) were another backward region from which travellers recoiled, finding there many dangers and few comforts. A visit to

14 This view of Genoa, from the *Supplementum Chronicarum* (1486), gives an impression of dense coastal settlement

Castile was like a journey into another world, where reluctant envoys from more civilized centres found themselves reduced to exchanging their horses for mules, killing and skinning their meat, living like gipsies and sleeping in the open. Inhabitants of these regions could not but be impressed by the evidence of prosperity to be found else-where. To a traveller from Castile the densely settled appearance of northern Italy in the 1430s was remarkable, and the coast from Savona to Genoa seemed 'like one continuous city, so well inhabited is it, and so thickly studded with houses.' A German pilgrim of the 1490s marvelled – even though he came from the region of Germany's leading city, Cologne – at the enormous numbers of people to be seen in Cairo. On the other hand southern England (relatively well populated by English standards), seen through the eyes of an Italian ambassador in 1500, presented the spectacle of a 'very thinly inhabited' country, with much land lying barren and waste.

The devastations of war added to the desolation of plague. The later Middle Ages was a period of more serious and protracted warfare than there had been in Europe for centuries. Though the disturbance caused by domestic strife might have only local or temporary effects, prolonged fighting over wide areas could dislocate a country's whole economy with serious long-term results. The destruction of war was long observable in both France and Bohemia. The Hundred Years' War between France and England (1337–1453) – to which the civil struggles between Burgundy and Orleans made such a notable contribution – reduced much of the French countryside to ruins, made conditions of life appalling, and had serious repercussions upon trade. After the conquest of Normandy, Henry V offered rewards for the taking of wolves and brigands and in 1423, several years after the Anglo-Burgundian occupation of Paris, when many inhabitants had fled from the city, it was estimated that there were 24,000 vacant houses there. The Hussite wars (1419–36) disrupted the Bohemian economy, diminished the standing of Prague, and reduced the population of the country from which many emigrants fled to the west (thereby giving rise, through a confusion, to the French term *bohémiens* for the gipsies, who appeared at about the same time).

Under the combined effects of depopulation and war the frontiers of civilization retreated. If the ability to travel unarmed against either man or beast is essentially a criterion of modern government, it is evident that even by medieval standards considerable areas at this time regressed for considerable periods. To European contemporaries the possibility of order without arms was unthinkable – which made fifteenth-century Egypt (like fourteenth-century China), where the inhabitants were to be observed travelling without weapons in town and country, a subject of astonishment. The western criterion of good order was the ability to travel unmolested when bearing gold or valuables, a state of affairs which was established, for instance, in the papal state in the 1420s by Martin V and towards the end of the century by Ferdinand and Isabella in Spain. Elsewhere such conditions were often lacking. The haunts of wolves as well as the lawlessness of men marked the limits of civilized life, and in the fifteenth century wolves appeared in capital cities. Their absence in England, where they became extinct in the reign of the first Tudor (though they lasted much longer in Scotland), was noteworthy to Continentals for whom things were different. And among those who contributed to the disorders of late medieval Europe were the ruined gentry, even men of princely blood, who under the stress of economic change and political dislocation took to a life of robbery and brigandage. Gentlemen beggars and knightly robbers became a familiar phenomenon in France and Germany, and even England (where on the whole disturbance was less lasting and disruptive) had its share of gentry robbery and violence. Robert de Caulincourt, sub-deacon of noble birth and a professed monk of St Quentin, who some years before 1434 had left his monastery and joined a band of *écorcheurs*, committing homicide, rapine and arson, changed his career in a way which was characteristic of many of his countrymen. And by no means all travellers through Austria were as fortunate as Pero Tafur, a Castilian hidalgo, who, on proclaiming to his would-be noble robbers that he was as poor as they were, was invited to join the entertainment, and so gained some useful guides to Vienna.

It will probably always be difficult to talk about the economic condition of Europe in this period as a whole. What is certain is that the contrasts of wealth and poverty, magnificence and misery, were enormous, and while we are no more able than contemporaries to strike an ultimate balance, we may notice as they did the most obvious differences and trends. Individuals, courts and particular regions prospered while others were in decline, and the poverty of the countryside – the ultimate basis of every sort of prosperity – was always somewhere observable. There were places in France which continued to bear the marks of late medieval agrarian devastation, centuries after the great reconstruction which began in the last decades of the fifteenth century. Although the decay of rural areas was reflected in city life, a higher proportion of the total population was living in urban surroundings than before. And contrasting with evidence of both urban and agrarian decay there were indubitable signs of wealth. Towns might profit at the expense of the countryside; individuals and corporations might gain while whole families

15 Jean Fouquet's miniature
of the building of
the temple of Jerusalem
shows the kind of scene
which could have been
observed in Vienna,
Ulm, Rouen or York,
and elsewhere

16 Views of Cologne
like that at right,
painted in 1489,
may be recognized
from the cathedral,
whose chancel, consecrated
in 1322, stood without its
nave for centuries

died out; new buildings took the place of old. Whereas the ambitious projects for rebuilding the cathedral of Siena were never completed after the interruption of 1348, there were other places which (not experiencing as did Italy a stylistic as well as a demographic revolution) found their building programmes promoted by offerings received in plague years. Such was the case at Ulm where, in the same decade that tax-payers received relief because town houses were falling into decay, a start was made on the minster. Mortality in cities might indirectly help new building schemes, and various German towns, such as Cologne, managed to undertake architectural improvements – enlarging churches, building new town halls. In Italy the scale of public and private building was such that it seemed by the middle of the century to Leone Battista Alberti (1404–72) to have transformed the country in a way comparable only to the period of high medieval building.

> What can be the reason, that just at this time all Italy should be fired with a kind of emulation to put on quite a new face? How many towns, which when we were children were built of nothing but wood, are now lately started up all of marble?

As a leading architectural practitioner, with the pride of Florentine

achievement in his blood, perhaps Alberti was liable to the understandable exaggeration which is born of high enthusiasm. Yet undoubtedly already by 1450 and still more by 1500 the cities of northern and central Italy had been transfigured by this architectural boom.

The parts of Europe which were the most conspicuously productive (economically and artistically) were also those with the largest numbers of people and the most active urban centres. It was Italy and the Low Countries which held this pre-eminence. Northern Italy – always far ahead, despite the commercial advances already evident in the cities of south Germany – dazzled contemporaries throughout the fifteenth century by its display of lavish expenditure and investment. Also impressive, but not on the same scale (or in the same ways), were the products of the extensive lands, stretching from Macon to Amsterdam, of the duchy of Burgundy. The great cities of Italy were larger than those elsewhere. Venice, which was described by the French chronicler Philip de Comines (c. 1447–1511) as 'the most triumphant city that I have ever seen', had in the last decade of the fifteenth century, when he saw it, something like 100,000 inhabitants. Naples was even larger and a number of other Italian cities, including Florence and Rome, exceeded the level of 40,000. North of the Alps there were as yet few cities which reached these proportions. Bruges and Ghent were probably nearer 30,000; Paris in the early fifteenth century – reduced to a fraction of her early fourteenth-century numbers – cannot have been much larger than Florence at the century's end. In Germany there was only a handful of cities of more than 20,000, and in England only one. Most urban life in the fifteenth century still had the close familiarity of a modern market town, such as Stratford-upon-Avon or Ely.

Although for many generations the search for antiquity, as well as for ecclesiastical promotion, led people to Rome, during the first formative years of the humanist movement far more roads led to Florence, and to Padua, Pavia or Ferrara. The state of Rome (like the state of Paris) depended largely upon the residence of its court, the absence of which spelt decline. Long before the period of papal residence at Avignon (1308–78) the popes had spent much time away from the Petrine city, but there is no doubt that this prolonged

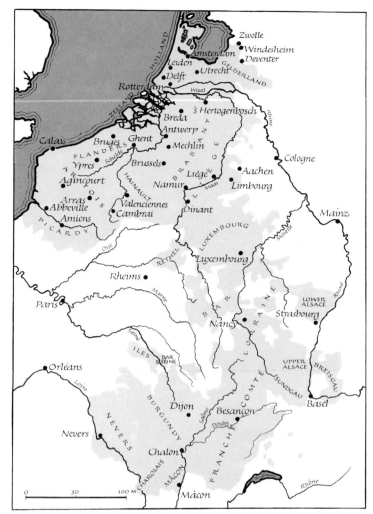

Zwolle
Windesheim
Deventer
Amsterdam
Leiden
HOLLAND
Delft
Utrecht
GELDERLAND
Rotterdam
Waal
Rhine
's Hertogenbosch
ZEELAND
Breda
Antwerp
Calais
Bruges
Ghent
Mechlin
Cologne
FLANDERS
Schelde
BRABANT
Ypres
Brussels
Liège
Aachen
ARTOIS
Agincourt
Namur
LIÈGE
Limbourg
Maas
Arras
HAINAULT
Valenciennes
Dinant
Mainz
Abbeville
Cambrai
Amiens
LUXEMBOURG
Moselle
PICARDY
Oise
RETHEL
Luxembourg
Rheims
Marne
BAR
Paris
Seine
Rhine
LORRAINE
LOWER ALSACE
Strasbourg
Nancy
ILES
SUNDGAU
BAR S. SEINE
UPPER ALSACE
BREISGAU
Orléans
Loire
FRANCHE COMTÉ
Basel
Dijon
Besançon
BURGUNDY
Saône
Doubs
Nevers
NEVERS
Chalon
CHAROLAIS
MÂCON
Rhône
0   50   100 M
Mâcon

17 The lands
of the duchy
of Burgundy
in the time of
Charles the Bold

absence reduced Rome to a condition from which it took long to recover. The grandeur of ancient buildings offset the paucity of the modern, and those who came to Rome, as did Petrarch in the mid-fourteenth century, from the bustle and thriving ecclesiastical commerce of Avignon, were as struck by the ruins of modernity as by those of antiquity.

The shepherd watches armed in the thickets, but fears the wolves less than the brigands. The ploughman ploughs in

27

armour, and pricks the ox with his spear. . . . Nothing happens here except by the force of arms. All night long the voice of the watchman re-echoes on the walls, and voices shouting 'To arms.'

Petrarch had personal experience for he was captured by bandits when he left Rome in 1341 after his spectacular coronation as poet.

Two generations later an English ecclesiastical lawyer used to get up at night to watch, from the window of his lodging near St Peter's, predatory wolves carrying off small dogs. 'O God, how much is Rome to be pitied!' Through the century many echoed Adam Usk's lament. Despite the restoration effected in the 1420s during Martin V's pontificate, the following decade brought pestilence, disturbance, renewed papal absence and, to a disdainful Florentine, the city of the popes was again reduced to 'a mere cow-pasture', where everyone went round dressed in peasant boots and cloaks.

18 Town and country never lay far apart in the fifteenth century, as can be seen from Fouquet's view of Notre Dame and the Seine in Paris ◀

19 Urban prosperity was particularly visible in some of the cities of Flanders where this street scene with shops was painted in the 1420s

While Rome suffered Florence throve. Already by the end of the fourteenth century Florence to the Florentines was a new Rome. 'What is it to be a Florentine, except to be, both by nature and law, a Roman citizen?' Salutati was not alone in regarding his city as preserving the heritage which was threatened by the decay of Rome, and what the Florentines recovered and created the rest of Europe was concerned to see, understand and inherit. The advance of humanism meant first and foremost the radiation of influences from Florence which could justifiably claim, in the early years of the fifteenth century, to be 'the mother of learning and of the arts.' The Florentines themselves went to Rome and further afield to collect the ingredients of their art and learning, but many more people came to Florence from other parts of Italy and northern Europe to learn Greek, collect manuscripts, make humanist contacts, and to admire the unparalleled achievements of Florentine art. Long before the time of Leonardo da Vinci (1452–1519) Florence had become, as he described it, 'a place of intercourse, through which many foreigners pass', admiring its celebrated works – Brunelleschi's dome, Ghiberti's bronze doors, the sculptures of Donatello. The discovery of Italy was the most conspicuous discovery of the century, and it certainly began with Florence. Just as the cathedral dome dominated the whole city, and as the city dominated Tuscany, so too there was a real sense in which – as its citizens so proudly believed – Florence dominated the international landscape of the Renaissance. 'The city herself stands in the centre, like a guardian and master; towns surround her on the periphery, each in its place. A poet might well speak of the moon surrounded by stars.' To Leonardo Bruni, eulogizing Florence early in the fifteenth century, it seemed that the city was set geometrically in its surroundings as the centre of a concentric order.

But Florence was not the only star in the international firmament of art and learning. Ferrara (whose university had an English rector in the 1440s) attracted a long succession of English students. Germans and others from the north came to pursue their studies at Padua and Pavia. The university of Padua, which was among the older Italian universities, came to be for the later fifteenth century what Paris and Oxford had been for earlier periods. It became the most significant university for intellectual advances. Padua's tolerance of outlook (which it owed to the patronage of Venice) already in 1409 enabled it to bestow a medical doctorate upon a Jew, and in the course of time attracted a wide variety of persons, ranging from the man of Halle, who came in 1396 to find a cure for his asthma, to Copernicus and Galileo. Moreover by the middle of the fifteenth century Rome had begun to change. The humanist patronage of Pope Nicholas V (1447–55) began the transformation which was to turn Rome into a cosmopolitan centre of art and learning, capable by the end of the century of rivalling and surpassing Florence. The Vatican library was founded; there were grandiose plans for rebuilding St Peter's and parts of the city; even a Florentine admitted that 'all the learned men of the world flocked to Rome of their own free will.' In the 1480s a future pope still had to betake himself to Florence to learn Greek, and throughout the century Rome failed to produce any artist of sufficient merit to work on the Sistine Chapel; but the focal point of the humanist world was shifting, all the same, significantly to Rome.

20, 21 An English friar in Rome about 1450 described the Colosseum as 'a temple . . . con-secrated to the sun and moon'. This drawing of it was done about 1480, when Rome under Sixtus IV was attaining its Renaissance leadership. Above, the new Vatican librarian, Platina, makes his submission to the pope

32

22–24 Three of the great Italian cities in the late fifteenth century. Left, the harbour of Naples. Below left, the Campanile and the Doge's Palace, Venice, in 1486. Below, a panorama of Florence about 1495

25 Antwerp, the leading northern harbour, in 1515. This view shows among the named landmarks, from left to right, a parish church (with spire), the town hall,

Other sorts of cosmopolitan influence emanated from the lands of the duchy of Burgundy. Ghent, Bruges and Ypres, whose commercial prosperity rested like that of Florence upon their textile industry, were also centres of art as well as of international trade. The dukes of Burgundy were richer than the kings of France and when, in 1420, Philip the Good (1419–67) moved his court from Dijon to the Low Countries, these cities gained the additional lustre of the greatest princely court of the west. Ducal patronage helped the Netherlands to enjoy a period of artistic and musical leadership. The praises of Jan van Eyck (c. 1390–1441) and Rogier van der Weyden (c. 1400–64) were sung in Italy as well as elsewhere, and Botticelli and Mantegna as well as Dürer were influenced by the *ars nova* of the north. Influences in painting flowed from north of the Alps to the south, as well as in the reverse direction. The composers of the Low Countries were the masters of European music for a century after 1420. And in matters of dress and fashion the Burgundian court was the arbiter of the century. 'As for the duke's court', John Paston the younger wrote home to his mother from Bruges in 1468, 'I heard never of none like to it, save King Arthur's court.' To be *à la mode* in

the cathedral, and the abbey of St Michael (at far right); on the Schelde River are barges and sea-going vessels

those days had more to do with Bruges than Paris. In the 1430s, even after a time of plague, dearth and disturbance, the commerce of Bruges was an impressive sight. For those with money there was everything to buy: spices from Alexandria, silks from the Levant, wine and fruit from Greece, fresh oranges and lemons from Castile. It was a place for luxurious living, but not a place for the poor. In the early part of the century Bruges was larger than London, and in the 1470s it was still described as a great international mart in which 'more merchandise is disposed of than in any other town of Europe.' But in the Netherlands as in Italy a change of orientation took place in the course of the century. When Dürer was lionized there in the 1520s there was still much to see and admire in Ghent and Bruges, but by then it was Antwerp which was the most vital centre. Bruges had long had trouble keeping its channel open to the sea. With the advent of larger ocean-going vessels it was unable to compete with the advantages of Antwerp, and through Antwerp were imported such objects as those which perhaps stirred Dürer more than anything else on this final journey – 'wonderful works of art' from Mexico.

There was unity and diversity, cosmopolitanism and provincialism, after the end as well as before the beginning of the fifteenth century. But in the course of a hundred years the forces of union and division changed in kind as well as in direction. In art and learning, and in language and politics, the separatist elements were more conspicuous by the end of the century than they had been when it began. Europe emerged from Christendom with consciously diversified loyalties.

In 1500 as in 1400, from Cambridge to Lisbon and from Abbeville to Prague, buildings were still being planned and constructed in the various regional styles of late Gothic. Throughout the fifteenth century as throughout the fourteenth, the demands of patrons called for the transmission of plans and architects as well as of craftsmen from one centre to another. But whereas about 1400 the predominating elements in the painting, sculpture and goldsmiths' works of different parts of Europe had so much in common that it is possible to speak of an 'international style', by 1500 enormous differences had developed between certain regions, and contemporaries were themselves becoming increasingly aware of divergences of style. Visitors to Florence already before the middle of the century and to other parts of Italy before its end, saw and learnt things which had no counterpart north of the Alps. If the prevailing style of European architecture was still predominantly Gothic, those who were most conscious of modernity were most explicitly reacting against what they understood to be the Gothic manner.

26, 27 French and Bohemian late Gothic: the west front of St Wulfran at Abbeville, begun in 1488, and the Vladislav Hall in Prague Castle, designed by Benedict Ried in 1493

28 Philip the Good, duke of Burgundy, receiving a translation of the *Chroniques de Hainaut*. The figures are authentic portraits including, on the duke's left, his son and heir Charles the Bold

The world of scholarship had also become more fragmented. Learning was still fundamentally international through the internationalism of Latin, and the Renaissance revival remained to the end more Latin than Greek. But at the same time as the intellectual leadership of Oxford and Paris passed to Italian centres, the proliferation of universities north of the Alps, together with the advance of the vernaculars, reflected some narrowing of horizons. Before the middle of the fourteenth century there were no universities north of Italy outside France and England. By the end of the fifteenth century there were twenty-three universities in this region, from Louvain and Mainz to Rostock, Cracow and Bratislava, and the number of universities in Europe as a whole had more than doubled. This

29 The university of Cracow
was founded in 1363
and revived by
King Ladislas Jagiellon in 1397.
The cloister of the library
(left) was built in the 1490s

30 Jacopo Bellini's drawing
of a university lecture (below)
was an imaginary scene
for a tomb of a professor;
its idealized order is unlikely
ever to have existed in practice

enormous expansion mirrors not only a great advance of education, but also some of the divisions of the time. The divided loyalties of the papal schism (1378–1417) and the long Anglo-French war both promoted new university foundations: Heidelberg and Cologne were among the German universities sponsored by the popes of Rome in order to reduce the advantage their Avignon rivals enjoyed in Paris; Poitiers and Caen were by-products of the English occupation of Paris. The new universities by no means ended the age-old peripateticism of learning. Nicholas of Cusa, Jacques Lefèvre d'Etaples and Lorenzo Valla ranged almost as far and as freely as their predecessors had done. The linguistic barriers of the learned were

38

those of dead, not living languages, and the very search for Greek knowledge was a stimulus to travel which contributed to the cosmopolitanism of certain places. More universities did mean, though, that for the rank and file of students learning no longer imposed the same necessity to travel. It became more possible and more common to study at home, and after the foundation of Leipzig in 1409 (itself the result of a German emigration from Prague which diminished the international character of that university), none of the new universities of Germany found it necessary to organize itself into different 'nations'.

31 Universities founded during the later Middle Ages

The most conspicuous divisions of the later Middle Ages did not derive from differences of language, but were certainly fostered by them. In this period the use of the vernaculars was notably extended, and linguistic developments contributed to political events. Even those strongholds of Latinity, the universities, made some concessions in this respect – as when the university of Paris provided French instruction for the barber-surgeons in the faculty of medicine. The vernaculars were coming into their own for official as well as familiar purposes. In England parliament was opened in English for the first time in 1362, and by the turn of the century the use of French or English had become a matter of taste in courtly circles. Various fifteenth-century governments (including those of England, Lombardy and Bohemia) provided for branches of their public records to be kept in the vernacular, and even the papal curia ceased to insist on its proceedings being conducted in Latin. The acquisition of modern languages was increasingly recognized as desirable, and these studies are themselves indications of the ways the world was facing. Englishmen provided for themselves with courses on French letter-writing, and the earliest printed books in England included aids to the French needed for courtly, diplomatic or commercial purposes. At a time when German merchants were still going to Italy to learn Italian business methods, Italians were discovering the value of an acquaintance with German. And at the highest levels linguistic considerations could be of major political importance. The most successful king of Bohemia in the fifteenth century was George of Poděbrady (1458–71) who was wholly Czech. Whereas his predecessor had had to be given a Czech tutor when he went to Prague from Vienna in 1453, Poděbrady managed to get along without becoming fluent in either German or Latin. Earlier, the use of Flemish formed part of the conciliatory policy of Philip the Bold, duke of Burgundy, towards Flanders when in the 1380s he entered into this inheritance, and later dukes learnt to speak Flemish although the language of their court was French.

'The generation of men', noted Leonardo da Vinci in a prophetic moment, 'shall come to such a pass as not to understand each other's speech; that is, a German with a Turk.' Prophecy apart, this had long been a truism, but it was one which was gaining new proportions. Differences of language were moving into a new context, acquiring greater significance. They were coming to be associated with other delineations, making a world more like the one with which we are familiar. Some discussions which took place between the English and French delegates at the Council of Constance showed the growing sense of these divergences. Anglo-French rivalry, woven on this occasion into acrimonious public argument, produced some significant criteria for regional pride. 'France contains many more and more notable provinces, many more episcopal churches, many more notable universities', claimed the French, asserting that in the spaciousness of their towns and cities, the number of their dioceses, clergy and people, they excelled the kingdom of England more than ten times. Numeration was the order of the day, and there was justice (as well as exaggeration) in these claims, for France probably had well over four times the population of England, as well as six universities against England's two. The English, however, were not to be outdone. They had more counties, more parish churches, old and noble kingdoms, and 'Britain itself is so broad and spacious that the distance from its north to its south, even if one travels a straight road, is, we all know, about eight hundred miles or forty legal days' journey.' France (they said) was not so vast, and the English could claim to be on a par with the Gallic nation 'whether a nation be understood as a race, relationship, and habit of unity, separate from others, or as a difference of language, which by divine and human law is the greatest and most authentic mark of a nation and the essence of it.'

The consciousness of geographical realities was growing, and so was the sense of numbers and vernaculars. Dignity, as these arguments show, was more a matter of multiplication than of unity. The more languages, the more kings and kingdoms, so (to older ways of thinking) the more glory. It was a matter of congratulation to the English, concerned to justify the multiplicity of their 'nation' as comparable to that of the French (which included Provence, Savoy and much of Lorraine), that they could claim to possess the distinct languages of Welsh, Irish, Gascon and Cornish, 'no one of which is understood by the rest.' Charles the Bold, duke of Burgundy (1467–77), whose ducal grandeur did not exclude aspiration to a royal title, is said to have remarked that he loved France so well that he would have liked her to have six kings instead of one. Rank and diversity in medieval thought were richer than unity.

It was long before vernacular riches were whittled away, with the help of printing, to single unities. It was as a whole a development which took place beyond this period. In the fifteenth century in fact, as the English claim at Constance indicates, vernaculars – for all their advances – might divide people more than unite them. 'There is no language which can be called the common tongue of Italy,' wrote Machiavelli about 1515, and from Dante until the sixteenth century, although Tuscan was steadily gaining ground, the form of Italian which should be the medium for literary expression remained a matter for discussion. Dante reckoned that there were more than a thousand varieties of Italian vernacular in his day. There was also diversity elsewhere. The Kentish housewife who, according to a famous story of Caxton's, when asked for *egges* by a visiting fellow countryman, said she knew no French, and who only understood when asked for *eyren*, exemplifies the same thing in England. Englishmen might not always recognize English.

'Who will understand the different languages?' asked Aeneas Silvius Piccolomini, four years before he became Pope Pius II (1458–64). 'Who will rule the diverse customs? Who will reconcile the English with the French, or join the Genoese to the Aragonese, or conciliate the Germans to the Hungarians and Bohemians?'

The forces of the day certainly seemed to be leading towards greater division, and the pope's failure to realize his great project of a crusade, like the earlier failure of Nicopolis, did indeed, as he so clearly saw, owe much to these forces of fission. To the popes who were still hoping for combined offensive action against the Turks, too much of the wealth and activity of the times was essentially centrifugal. Perhaps – since the past is clearer than the future – it is always easier to believe in disintegration than in regeneration. Although, as we shall see, the fifteenth century produced optimists as well as pessimists, there were few contemporaries who were aware of the most dynamic ways in which the direction of their world was changing. For the few who saw the possibilities of expansion in the west there were far more who continued to think solely in terms of the old Mediterranean world and the contracting horizons of the east.

In 1466 Leo of Rožmital, Catholic brother-in-law of the Bohemian Hussite king, who had set out in November 1465 on a diplomatic tour of European courts, rode with his companions beyond Compostella to the tip of Cape Finisterre. One of the party recorded their impressions. 'One sees nothing anywhere but sky and water. They say that the water is so turbulent that no one can cross it and no one knows what lies beyond. It is said that some had tried to find out what was beyond and had sailed with galleys and ships, but not one of them returned.' Nearly twenty years after this Felix Faber, a Dominican of Ulm in Swabia, wrote up a lengthy account of his two pilgrimages to the Holy Land in which he explained to his readers how the 'infallible truth of Holy Scripture proves by its testimonies that Jerusalem is in the middle of the world.' Scripture, history and experience made it impossible to believe in the existence of the antipodes. There was no land beyond the ocean and in any case, 'it is impossible to reach the other side of the globe because of the vast extent of the ocean, which it is impossible for any of our shipping to traverse.'

These contemporaries belonged to a world which was already becoming outmoded, though many generations passed before it was replaced. Six years before Rožmital and his company made their trip to Finisterre, Prince Henry the Navigator died in the town that he had founded, the Vilo do Infante near Cape St Vincent. Under his enlightened guidance during the previous forty years Portuguese explorers had discovered over 2,000 miles of the African coastline, from Ceuta to Sierra Leone; they had already sailed far into the open sea, to Madeira, the Azores, the Cape Verde Islands. In the same years that Faber was investigating the sights of Jerusalem, Columbus was proving to himself by a voyage to the Portuguese fortress of Mina on the Gulf of Guinea that the torrid zone was in fact inhabitable,

32, 33 Among the leading members of the Portuguese royal family who appear in the panel by Nuno Gonçalves are (kneeling) King Afonso V (1438–81), for whom the picture was painted, and (the elderly man above him, with moustache) his uncle Prince Henry, nicknamed 'the Navigator' for his organization and direction of overseas expeditions. Little now remains of the buildings on the promontory near Sagres, where the prince started constructing a new town in 1443, but the sixteenth-century plan (below left) suggests something of their layout. Prince Henry had a residence, study and chapel there, but his ships were fitted out and sailed from Lagos

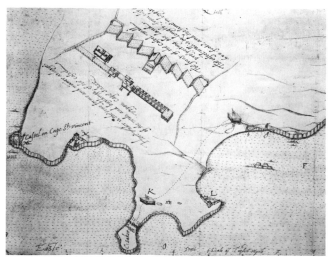

and by 1485 he had presented the first version of his extravagant plans to John II of Portugal. Columbus was himself at Lisbon when in December 1488 Bartholomew Dias returned in triumph from the Cape of Good Hope. And in 1497–8 Vasco da Gama, taking in an enormous sweep of the South Atlantic and making the longest voyage that any European vessel had hitherto achieved in the open sea, crossed the Indian Ocean to Calicut and returned the following year with three-quarters of his company and the first cargo of spices. The king of Portugal grandly added to his titles that of 'Lord of the conquest, navigation and commerce of Ethiopia, Arabia, Persia and India.' A new era of expansion had begun.

34 The world-map, *c.* 1489, of Henricus Martellus – a German cartographer who worked in Florence at the end of the fifteenth century – though it follows Ptolemy in the delineation of Asia, has abandoned the concept of a land-locked Indian Ocean, and shows the seaway to the east which had recently been opened by the Portuguese

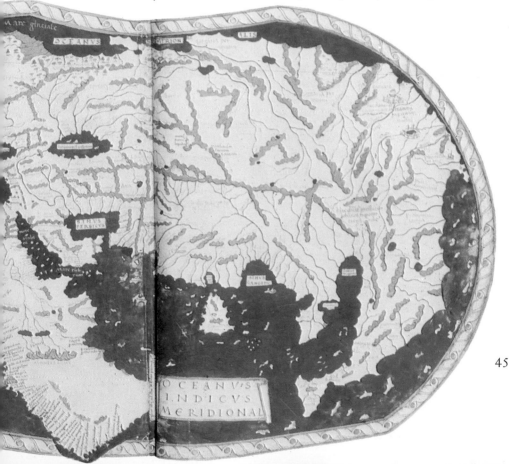

45

Men of learning in the Middle Ages were not accustomed to the idea that knowledge could be outdated. To their thinking the older the fact the better the fact and, with their great respect for the weight of authority, facts and opinions were not clearly differentiated. It was not only that new ideas and discoveries took time to become known, but there is also a sense in which new ideas demand new minds to receive them. If it was long before the old world fully took the measure of the new, one of the reasons must be that in the fifteenth century and later many people continued to rely on old ideas and to think of the new west in terms of the old, imperfectly known east. Some of the conceptions of Columbus did not differ greatly from his most studied source, Pierre d'Ailly's *Imago Mundi* (*c.* 1410), which in its turn had completely ignored fourteenth-century discoveries of China. And Columbus himself, visionary and dogmatic, died in 1506 without recognizing the true nature of what he had found.

But not all contemporaries were insensible to the geographical revolution of their time. Already the intellectual horizons of the day were beginning to be affected, and if those north of the Alps suffered a disadvantage in that they had in a sense to discover Italy before they could discover the new world, there were others besides Italians who quickly began to revise their views in the light of exploration. A professor of Cracow, John of Glogau (d. 1507) pointed out that the discovery of Ceylon disproved the old idea of an uninhabitable torrid zone. Giannozzo Manetti (1396–1459), writing *On the Dignity and Excellence of Man*, acclaimed the gradual advance in methods of navigation in his time, which seemed to be almost miraculous. 'They have lately striven to penetrate beyond previously navigable limits, where we hear that there have been discovered many cultivated and inhabited islands, hitherto completely unknown.' Peter Martyr d'Anghiera (1459–1526), who was present at Barcelona in 1493 when the Castilian court received Columbus after his first voyage, had already in 1494 resolved to write a history of what he saw to be a new world. His imagination was fired by the vastness of the discoveries. 'Behold, how posterity will see the Christian religion extended! How far it will be possible to travel amongst mankind! Neither by word of mouth nor by my pen can I express my sentiments concerning these wondrous events.' Peter Martyr was not alone in looking to the future in the west. Excitement was also stirring the recipients of his letters in Italy. And Antonio Galateo of Ferrara (1444–1517), who lived long enough to dismiss his own doubts about the Portuguese circumnavigation of Africa, and to be able to laugh at those who believed that the ocean could not be traversed, expressed pride in the age he was born in.

> All glory to those valiant men and most deserving of our commemoration and well deserving of posterity who dared to entrust themselves to an unknown and boundless sea, who dared to penetrate that vast void of nature. They have taught us that there is nothing that is impossible for man.

The ocean had been opened and with it the sphere of potential human endeavour. The fact and the realization of it were both to transform Europe into the world we know, and the landscape of 1500 already seems more recognizable than that of 1400. The first important steps towards geographical and intellectual reorientation had taken place, and Christians of the west had discovered new ways of approaching old questions of the east. The whole of the future rested upon a new equilibrium. A period had started which is only now coming to an end.

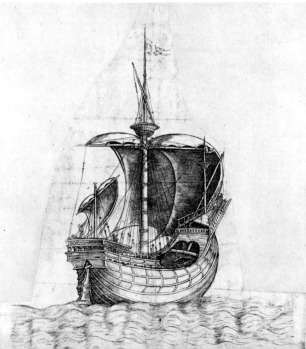

35 The design of ships was improved in various ways in the fifteenth century. The carrack, which was in general use at the time of the discovery of America, was the result of a revolution in rigging. Besides a large mainmast it carried a small foremast and a lateen sail aft, which added greatly to its sailing qualities

36 An ambassadorial leave-taking, set by Carpaccio in the ceremonial of late fifteenth-century Venice

II NEWS AND KNOWLEDGE

Know you not, when a letter comes from a king, how sweet it is to go and hear that letter?

SAN BERNARDINO OF SIENA (d. 1444)

One half of the world does not know how the other half is behaving.

PHILIP DE COMINES

Since the fifteenth century the community of Europe has both enlarged and contracted, grown apart and drawn together. It has changed particularly strikingly in its ability to communicate. Already between the end of the fourteenth century and the early years of the sixteenth, some remarkable changes had taken place in the methods of communication, and for some purposes the Continent was effectively made smaller. Although the full impact of these changes was not realized until the fifteenth century was over, new processes had been devised for making a world which was more united in news and knowledge, even though it might be more divided in politics and opinion.

In this period, as before and after, there were various levels and forms of communication, each with its own speed. The rate of international governmental communication was not the same as the untraceable travel of rumour and disease; the speed at which ordinary individuals journeyed was more leisurely than either. Ideas and styles, whether transplanted haphazardly or deliberately, crossed frontiers more slowly than any persons, public or private. Corporations and individuals, the rulers and the ruled, the learned and the unlearned, in this century as throughout the Middle Ages lived in different worlds of communication. Knowledge which might be common property in one world seeped only gradually and imperceptibly, if at all, into the consciousness of the other. The localism of the unlearned as much as the internationalism of the learned was always characteristic of medieval society.

By the end of the fifteenth century some revolutionary innovations had begun to transform the links which connected the inhabitants of Europe on these different levels. Knowledge was enabled more readily to cross the barriers of class and privilege as well as those of language. The introduction of an international posting system during the last years of the century showed the way to accelerated communications, capable of influencing the lives of subjects, as well as the decisions of rulers. The invention of printing, while on the one hand it strengthened the forms and divisions of the vernaculars, on the other made possible the dissemination of common knowledge throughout the length and breadth of Europe. Ideas which, though individuals might carry them fast and far, remained restricted in the days of manuscript learning by the limitations of textual dissemination, became capable in the days of printing of burgeoning into an international movement in the space of a few years. Wycliffe and Hus were separated from Luther by a technical discovery as well as by time, circumstance and conviction.

The possession of news and up-to-date information has always been an aspect of power. Perhaps this was particularly evident in the later Middle Ages. Those who were privileged in this way were most usually governments and corporations – whose organizations might benefit individuals – and occasionally powerful persons emerged, who competed with this aspect of public authority. The messenger services of the papal curia, of the kings of Aragon and England, the republic of Venice, the university of Paris and elsewhere, were already important government departments served by numerous officials early in the fourteenth century. Some of such services moreover, such as those which linked Regensburg, Nuremberg, Augsburg, Ulm and other German towns, were beginning to approximate to public messenger services by making some provision for the sending of private as well as official letters. They could also, on occasion, achieve journeys of remarkable speed. In 1302 the news of the battle of Courtrai in Flanders took only seven days to reach Boniface VIII in Rome, and in 1406 Thomas della Croce left London on diplomatic business on 19 March and arrived six days later in

Milan, having travelled over six hundred miles (including the Channel and the Alps) at an average speed of one hundred miles a day. Such journeys were most exceptional feats, dependent upon unusual favour of circumstances. Even for official purposes a far more normal rate was that of an exchange of letters which took place between the pope and the English king in 1422, lasting exactly two months between Rome and London, with replies by return.

Gossip is not easily divorced from news, and diplomacy depends upon report as well as upon fact. The development of diplomatic procedures, in which (as in so much else in this period) Italy led the way, was closely attached to the need to keep an ear to the ground for information of every description. By the 1450s the leading powers of Italy had developed among themselves an established network of permanent embassies, and one of the chief functions of resident ambassadors – who before the end of the century were being appointed outside Italy and by other powers – was to act as news-agents for their governments, to listen attentively and report comprehensively the chatter of their locality. This function was naturally assisted in Italy by the relatively short distances which made it feasible to expect and to receive daily doses of ambassadorial gossip.

37 Cairo, where a Venetian embassy is here seen arriving, seemed to western visitors a city of prodigious population and extent. Venice was linked to Cairo and Alexandria by regular sailings

Between Florence and Milan, Venice and Naples, diplomatic exchanges – weighty or flighty – could pass frequently without incurring vast difficulties or expenditure. An ambassador whose pen flowed as easily as a courier might ride could over the months make the written word compete with the ridden miles. One active Venetian resident in Rome in the early years of the sixteenth century sent off 472 dispatches within a single year. The case was different, however, with more distant exchanges. When Ferdinand of Castile-Aragon demanded, in an impatient moment, daily missives from his resident ambassador in London he was not asking for the impossible, but it would have been a very expensive request to implement. To keep such contacts between London and Toledo would, the ambassador himself calculated, have needed at least sixty couriers constantly on the roads. Italy was ahead of the rest of Europe in the conquest of space travelled, as well as pictorially represented space.

Powerful commercial corporations, like governments, were the privileged possessors of international news. The widespread interests of the Teutonic Knights were matched by the international coverage of their agents and reporters; and the great trading companies of Italy and Germany were in a position to vie with governments by virtue of their control of information as well as by their financial capacities. The Florentines, Gregorio Dati remarked without exaggeration about 1407–8, 'have spread their wings over the world and have news and information from all its corners.' The international scale of the business of the great merchant houses of Florence was indeed impressive in its extent. Even during the period of their misfortunes and exile the Alberti had representatives in ten cities of England, the Low Countries, France, Germany and Italy. The Medici, whose banking capacities were the most substantial of their day, had seven or eight branches and employed between forty and fifty factors throughout western Europe – and in the previous century the operations of the Bardi and Peruzzi had exceeded even these limits. In France the great merchant Jacques Cœur (who made a gigantic fortune in Mediterranean trade which was confiscated by the crown when his fall was engineered in the 1450s) created his own private pigeon-post to keep in touch with his numerous widespread

38 Jacques Cœur's great *hôtel* at Bourges, of which this is the courtyard, was begun in 1443 and was still not entirely completed – though already in occupation – when it was seized by the king in 1451. The holes for Cœur's carrier pigeons are still visible in the attics

agents – a system which he may well have imitated from the Arab world, where it had long excited the wonder and admiration of westerners.

In the later part of the fifteenth century contemporaries were becoming more aware of the needs of communication. And they made use of new techniques to improve them. In the 1480s gunpowder was being used to widen the Alpine passes in Austria, and by this time the advantages of post-riding were being appreciated and utilized. Regular courier exchanges at considerably accelerated speeds were made possible by the establishment of chains of equestrian change-posts to provide for relay riding. This amounted to a technical invention in the west, though travellers to the east had long since remarked on the amazing communications maintained

39 A pass in the Alps, drawn by Dürer in 1495 after his first visit to Italy. Crossing the Alps was an ordeal for medieval travellers; Adam Usk, who braved the St Gotthard in an ox-cart in 1402, was blindfolded 'lest I should see the dangers of the pass'

within the Mongol empire by means of a system of messengers and change-posts. Ruy González de Clavijo, who journeyed through Asia in 1404–5 on a mission from Castile to the court of Timur (Tamerlane), was as impressed as Marco Polo had been by the supply of post-horses and messengers on the roads all the way to Samarkand, which enabled news to come from every province in a few days. 'In truth it would scarcely be believed, unless it was actually seen, the distances which these fellows travel, each day and night.' When fifteenth-century governments took steps to institute this system, a comparable sense of wonder was aroused among contemporaries who respected the power of speed.

The first government to adopt the new system was that of Louis XI of France (1461–83). The posting services and routes which he established seem to have been designed to meet the special demands of foreign and domestic affairs, rather than forming part of a general planned network. His rapid couriers (reported to number 234 at his death) riding day and night had, however, transformed royal communications, and the impact of the achievement is reflected in the retort of the outspoken preacher Olivier Maillard who, on receiving a threat of drowning from the outraged king, replied that he would get to heaven more quickly by water than his monarch would with his post-horses. A more far-reaching and permanent system was that which was created over the turn of the century to provide for the extensive needs of Habsburg family diplomacy. The alliances of Maximilian I (1493–1519) and his descendants stretched from Austria, Carinthia and the Tyrol to Italy, Burgundy, the Netherlands and Castile, and produced highly ambitious schemes for governmental intercommunications. Maximilian's own marriage with Mary of Burgundy (d. 1482) brought his house the rich Burgundian inheritance, while the double marriage of 1496 between his children and those of Ferdinand and Isabella of Castile-Aragon allowed him, soon afterwards, to expect the combined Spanish inheritance. Under the direction of Maximilian's post-master from the 1490s onwards a posting system was developed to link these various regions.

The earliest international link in the Habsburg postal chain was that established between the courts of Innsbruck and Milan after the marriage between Maximilian and Bianca Sforza in 1494. Already

40–42 Three individuals who were associated with the posting systems of the later fifteenth century: Louis XI of France, Maximilian I, and his wife, Bianca Maria Sforza

two generations earlier the Milanese government had placed a high premium upon rapid communications, and under Habsburg influence these were extended beyond the Alps. The journey from Milan to Worms was in 1495 reduced to 6 days 16½ hours, an overall average speed of 60 miles a day with a rate of more like 90 on the easiest, least mountainous stretches. Another important postal connection was the one between Maximilian's court at Innsbruck and that of his son Philip in the Netherlands, at Brussels or Mechlin; and Philip in his turn needed good communications with Castile, which he claimed in the name of his wife Joanna in 1504. By 1505 posting links had been formed between Innsbruck, Milan and Vienna, Augsburg, Worms and the Netherlands, and it was possible to envisage a series of routes from Brussels to Innsbruck, Paris, Blois, Lyons, Granada and Toledo, worked out on average daily speeds of about 80–95 miles in summer and 65–80 in winter. Brussels could be thought of as separated from Paris by 44–54 hours, from Lyons by 4–5 days, from Innsbruck by 5½–6½ days and from Toledo by 13 or 14. Though some parts of this time-table long remained mainly theoretical, and it is doubtful how frequently or effectively such contacts were maintained, a new speed and a new form of communications had in fact been created. It became feasible for the first time in medieval Europe to communicate regularly over long distances at rates of about 80–90 miles a day; what had once been a rare feat was made a repeatable performance. Soon after 1500 posting was developing more widely in Europe and an important advance had been made in the conquest of space. The possible rate of long-distance travel had been doubled and the size of the Continent, at least in some areas, for some official purposes, had been reduced.

Yet this revolution in communications was essentially limited in its effects, in that it was essentially governmental and commercial. It was not until later that the exchange of private as well as of official correspondence became possible at the new speeds. And while the sending of private news remained subject to numerous hazards, most ordinary travellers continued to journey at the old slow rates, reckoning at best on 30–40 miles a day. 'My dearest Giovanni, each time you write to say that you have not had a letter from me it is like a knife-blow, for I have written to you six times in the last year,' Machiavelli wrote to his nephew in Pera (a quarter of Constantinople) in 1516. The frustrations of private correspondence were still much the same as they had been 150 years earlier, when Petrarch was annoyed to discover that three letters, which he had written to Boccaccio over seven months before, were still in the possession of the man to whom he had entrusted them. And it was by no means only the letters of literary celebrities which were inclined to get lost in the post. While urgent official missives might pass with relative security from London to Rome in a matter of thirteen days, scholars, clerics and pilgrims (with unofficial exchanges of letters) continued to reckon on double or treble that time – and there was still reason to be thankful if they reached their destinations at all. The priest Richard Torkington in 1518, like the canon lawyer Adam Usk in 1402, took between six and seven weeks to cover the distance between a Channel port and Rome – somewhat longer than Matthew Paris had needed in the thirteenth century. The periods allowed for the maturing of bills of exchange show the unhurried rates of normal business transfers: three months for the double communication between Florence and London, two between Florence and Bruges. Long after the novel achievements of Louis XI's post-horses, long-distance travel continued for most people to be what it had always been – the rate of an individual and a horse going as far as physical endurance and a day's light would conveniently carry them. So while for top-level government purposes Europe, by the beginning of the sixteenth century, was not much more than a fortnight long and broad, for most ordinary purposes it remained very much greater than this.

The demand for diversion, as well as the need for news, made letters and messengers important events. In the days when official reporting was rare and uncertain, those who enjoyed access to government sources or who purveyed good news were privileged and well-rewarded persons. Philip de Comines, who earned two hundred marks for giving Louis XI the news of the great Burgundian defeat at Morat in 1476, describes the courtiers' competition to obtain the first authentic reports of that event. And when Machiavelli, near the end of his life, was sent on a minor diplomatic mission to the

Franciscans of Carpi, he derived a good deal of amusement by making play with the friars' naïve deference to his official messenger. 'I must tell you,' he wrote to his friend Francesco Guicciardini at Modena, 'how, when the crossbow-man arrived with the letter and bowed down to the ground and said that he had been sent expressly, and in haste, they all came to life with such bowings and scrapings and general hubbub that everything seemed turned upside down.' The teasing envoy was not above elaborating upon the contents of the letter to dramatize the situation (and himself) still further, and wrote back to Guicciardini asking him next time he sent such a messenger to 'let him gallop and arrive covered in sweat, and startle the people here out of their wits.'

The arrival of news meant incomparably more in the fifteenth century than it does now. It had all the savour of rarity and if, added to that, there was also the spice of uncertainty, truth was always very relative for those who had few means of verification. 'There will be rumours upon rumours. . . . Rumours from the east, from the west; from all sides rumour after rumour.' It was not for nothing that rumour was still being personified in the sixteenth century, for (as Savonarola understood) it played a large part in the lives of everyone, governments included. Petrarch in 1363 nearly lost both the canonries he already held, as well as the promise of a new one, because a report of his death which was circulating had been credited when it reached Avignon. It was one of the hazards of daily life that death – even one's own – often took place *in absentia*. Petrarch himself enjoyed the perhaps mixed pleasure of writing a reply to his own obituary, and while particularly long-lived celebrities (such as Philip the Good, who had been duke of Burgundy for nearly half a century when he died aged 71 in 1467) must have grown accustomed to hearing of their own decease, many others of humbler station arrived home (as did Guicciardini in 1513) to find that death had taken off a near relation faster than they had been able to travel.

Officials, just as much as private individuals, could not afford to disregard popular reports, for even after the improvement of official communications, rumour might still outrun the fastest courier. 'Tongues carry tales to every place/Much faster than a coach could

43, 44 Francesco Guicciardini (1483–1540) and Niccolo Macchiavelli (1469–1527)

race,' as Sebastian Brant truly commented near the end of the century. Events might often catch up with gossip as they did, for instance, in 1483 when the citizens of York enjoyed the advantage of receiving a trustworthy report of the death of their sovereign, Edward IV, three days before the king died and eight days before the heir to the throne (who was then at Ludlow) learnt of his accession. Unofficial news must frequently have preceded official announcements, and sage recipients were cautious (especially where news from distant parts was concerned) in their estimates of first hearings. So Pius II describes how when he was at Naples in 1456 rumour reported the siege of Belgrade by a large Turkish force. King Alfonso began at once to consider what should be done. Nothing, counselled the future pope, in view of the nature of these wars and seeing that at 'this very moment, while we are speaking, either the enemy or the Hungarians are in flight and we shall presently have the report.' Sure enough a week later a letter was received from Hungary describing the Christian victory, and 'the information was so precise that no further evidence could be required.'

59

45–47 Female Negro slaves, such as the one at left, were not uncommon in the time of Cosimo de' Medici (1434–64). It was during the life of Cosimo (centre) that the great wealth of the

Rumour, plague, and the processes of printing all followed the routes of trade. There was an internationalism of trade as well as of religion and learning, and trading connections always played an important part in the transmission of both techniques and ideas. While certain regions were linked by regular commercial enterprises, like the annual fleets which sailed northwards from Venice to Bruges and Southampton and southwards from the Hanseatic towns to the salt-pans of the Bay of Bourgneuf, consumer demands also connected more distant areas. The bowstaves used by English archers at Agincourt in 1415 may have come from the Carpathian mountains, and luxury commodities from Italy (such as saffron or silk) were taken to eastern Europe, to Hungary, Bulgaria, Serbia. In the other direction one of the important imports was human. Slavery was an accepted institution in the Mediterranean regions in the fifteenth century, and the sale of Tartars, Moors, Turks, Russians, Circassians, even Greeks, was a familiar sight in the markets of Aragon, Italy and southern France. These 'domestic enemies', *femmine bestiali* (as one of their mistresses called them), were common in Italian households – Cosimo de' Medici owned four in 1457 – and this was one of the ways in which the society of the south differed from that of the north. The Black Death, which reached Sicily in October 1347 from the ports of the Crimea, travelled the same route as many slaves. Reflecting the rates of transportation of rats and fleas

Medici reached its peak. The Medici Bank in Milan (above), designed by Michelozzo and finished in 1461, was one of the first Renaissance buildings in that city

as well as of humans, the disease itself demonstrated the commercial integration of western Europe. It arrived in England – having devastated France – in the summer of 1348, reached Sweden and Poland towards the end of 1349, and in the course of three years had infected the whole of the west with the exceptions of Bohemia and Hungary. The travels of rumour and disease, associated with trade, reveal the intercommunications of the humble which are otherwise untraceable. Even at such a level there was a community of some sort which we might now label 'European'.

Although some contemporaries were more conscious of their advances than of their age-old limitations, their world remained, through restrictions of transport, both large and divided. The vast distances of European space continued to hamper business and correspondence throughout the sixteenth century and later. Difficulties of communication also influenced European relationships with east and west. Hungary and Poland, despite the links which existed, were relatively remote; measured by the speed of papal financial transactions, the distance from Rome to Cracow might seem six times greater than that to either London or Bruges. The obstacles which impeded eastern affairs were shown only too clearly by the time which it took for one of the most notable events of the century to become known throughout the west. Constantinople fell, after a siege of nearly two months, on 29 May 1453.

61

Significantly it was Venice that first received news of this calamity, but not until a whole month after it had happened. The council which heard the report on 29 June was so overcome that nobody present even asked to see a copy of the report. Rome first learnt of the disaster – relayed from Venice – nine days later, on 8 July, and Aeneas Silvius Piccolomini, longing for it to be false, had the news at Graz four days after that. Such indeed was the prevalence of false reporting and the power of wishful thinking that even then there were still persons in Rome and Geneva who refused to believe that the disaster had taken place. And it was not until August, two months after its occurrence, that the fate of the Emperor Constantine XI and his city was generally known in the capitals of the west.

Such time-lags and such disbelief not only display the impediments under which contemporary governments and diplomacy laboured. They also show something of the vagaries of communications to which knowledge, even the general knowledge of the most educated concerning the most outstanding events, was customarily subjected. It was important too, for the reorientation of Europe eastwards to westwards, that the contacts established by the new oceanic routes could, for all the immensity of the distances involved, compete in point of time with the existing communications in other directions.

48 Joan of Arc being tied to the stake, from a French miniature of 1484. Joan was burnt on 30 May 1431, but the news of her death was still scarcely credited at the imperial court in Constantinople near the end of 1432

Columbus reached Dominica on his second voyage in 1493 three weeks after his departure from the Canaries, five weeks after leaving Cadiz; his return voyage in 1496 took only seven weeks. Knowledge of events in eastern Europe might not be received in western centres much more quickly, as was demonstrated in 1453, or four years later when the first news of the king of Hungary's execution of Laszlo Hunyadi arrived in Milan a whole month after its occurence. Exchanges the other way about could take even longer, as a French visitor to Constantinople discovered in 1432, when he startled the imperial court with an authentic account of the fate of Joan of Arc who had been burned at Rouen over eighteen months before. Measured by the limitations of contemporary communications, America might sometimes seem as near as eastern Europe. And it was not otherwise with the sea-route to the east which could compete in time, as well as rivalling the costs of the older, shorter land-routes. Owing to sailing problems in the Red Sea and the various necessary trans-shipments, this route to India took about $17\frac{1}{2}$ months. The Cape route took about twenty. Thanks to the rivalry of sea-routes with land-routes, as well as to the rivalry of Christian with Turk, Europeans could establish surer communications by oceanic travel to the west than those which they already had with the east by land.

Some forms of knowledge which were deliberately propagated over considerable areas of Europe in this period not only enjoyed none of the advantages of official methods of communicating, but were themselves proscribed by the authorities which maintained such services. The effective dissemination of a corpus of heretical opinions depended upon transporting suspect texts, as well as ideas, from one area to another, and a notable transfusion of this kind which took place in the later Middle Ages was that which transferred the bulk of Wycliffe's writings from England to Bohemia. Wycliffe died in 1384, after his works but not his person had been condemned. Within a generation his major writings had been taken to Prague where their contents, grafted on to the indigenous Bohemian re-forming movement and utilized by the Czechs for their own pur-poses, had momentous results for Hus as well as the Hussites. The condemnation of Hus at the Council of Constance in 1415 was preceded by the condemnation of Wycliffe, and before the first thirty years of the fifteenth century were over Wycliffe's name was being used as an abuse for different heretics in many parts of Europe.

The Bohemians' acquisition of Wycliffite texts – which stemmed from existing contacts between the universities of Prague and Oxford – was a slow process, partly because of the difficulties of access once the English authorities were alerted to heresy, partly because of the sheer labours of copyists and travellers. Before 1398, when Hus copied and glossed them, Prague possessed three of Wycliffe's philosophical works. Hus's close associate, Jerome of Prague, drawn to Oxford about 1399 by Wycliffe's fame, spent about two years there in the course of which he transcribed two important works which he took home with him, together with some other of the master's writings. As time went on, however, Oxford became a dangerous centre for visitors with such interests. Two Bohemians who spent some time in England a few years later, collecting more texts and paying a pious visit to Wycliffe's tomb in Leicestershire, did their main copying at Lollard hide-outs in two country villages of Northamptonshire and Gloucestershire, and their call at Oxford (where they corrected their texts) was probably not prolonged. Thanks to such labours, by 1410, when the archbishop of Prague made a public bonfire of Wycliffe's writings, the Czechs possessed most of the important works of the late Oxford master. Moreover, as time went on it was not only the Latin works of the English heresiarch which were acquired by the Bohemians. Czech interest in and admiration for Wycliffe brought them also some works of his epigoni – texts which have likewise in a number of cases survived only through preservation in the centres of eastern Europe. Such were the links and the sense of community formed between heretics of east and west that English Lollard works might be translated into Latin, as well as Latin ones into Czech, to inspire and serve the cause of Bohemian associates.

The personal connections between heretics in England and Bohemia did not last significantly beyond a generation. But the missionary efforts of devoted early followers who went to great lengths to spread knowledge of his life and works, extended Lollard reverence for Wycliffe to distant foreign parts with long-lasting effect. The Czechs derived much encouragement from a letter, sealed with the common seal of the university of Oxford, directed to all members of the universal church, which sang the praises of Wycliffe's life, opinions and writings, as the peerless son of his university. After his return home Jerome of Prague got himself into trouble in Vienna for activities which appear to have included disseminating Wycliffe's ideas in Hungary and Austria. About the same time the masters of Vienna sent warning to the bishop and chapter of Zagreb that there were people in their diocese who had become infected by Wycliffe's teaching when they were in Prague. Down to the time of his death in 1455 one of the leading figures in Hussite affairs was the Englishman Peter Payne, who had resumed in Prague a career which his Wycliffism had terminated in Oxford.

The inspiration derived from a sense of shared aspirations was able to communicate itself, even in a heretical underworld, far afield across Europe. 'The church of Christ in Bohemia greets the church of Christ in England,' Hus wrote in 1411, returning thanks to the Englishman Richard Wyche for his letter of sympathy and exhortation – a letter which had brought such comfort that Hus had translated it into Czech for the benefit of a congregation at a public sermon. It was the theme of a great common cause which transcended barriers of geography or language. 'You therefore, Hus, beloved brother in Christ,' Wyche had written, 'since the distance of lands cannot separate those whom the love of Christ truly binds together . . . labour as a good soldier of Jesus Christ.' Persecution could not prevent such fraternization. The world seemed small to those who believed they could transform it. Nearly forty years later an ardent Polish admirer of Wycliffe penned some vernacular verses to his far-reaching fame.

> You Poles and you Germans,
> Men of all nations,
> If you waver – be it in speech
> And any word of script –
> Wycliffe will tell you truth.

Though the cause – even the purely philosophical cause – was a lost one at Cracow in 1449 (as Master Andreas Galka Dobczyn discovered to his cost when his Wycliffite books were confiscated), others elsewhere were still working actively for the internationalism of belief which he proclaimed.

Hussite propaganda, which by the 1430s reached as far as Spain and Scotland (where a Czech was burned by the bishop of St Andrews in 1433), included considerable efforts to join forces with the long-established Waldensian communities of Germany. These associations had begun early in the century and an important agent in some ambitious plans of the 1450s was Frederick Reiser, a Swabian Waldensian turned Hussite. He headed a mission sent by the Hussites to Germany, for which he was consecrated bishop by Peter Payne. Reiser's title expressed the comprehensive nature of the heretical programme: 'Frederick by the grace of God bishop of the faithful in the Roman church who reject the Donation of Constantine'. In the following decade when the Unity of the Czech Brethren were searching far and wide for a church which could provide for their apostolic succession, these connections went further and some of the Bohemians had their own orders confirmed by the Waldensian bishop, Stephen of Basel.

The world of these heretics, like the world of the universities from which their doctrines stemmed and where some of them were trained, and like the world of the church whose workings they deplored, was international in the sense that it was not limited by vernaculars or kingdoms. They shared common purposes and aspired to the formation of a purified church of European dimensions.

Richard Wyche, Peter Payne and their associates and successors were well aware, for all the divergences of unorthodox opinion, of the advantages of pooling grievances and drawing together. In order to do so they developed over wide areas the communications which were vital for such co-operation. By the transmission of texts and the missionary activity of individuals, the Hussites kept alive through the fifteenth century those heretical interconnections which began with the export of Wycliffite writings to Bohemia.

Another comparable transference which began to take place in the fifteenth century has had much more lasting effects. This was the extension from Italy to the rest of Europe of the ideas of Italian humanists. Here too the spread of ideas went with the acquisition of texts, but in this case the dissemination was helped by two different innovations, both of which promoted contemporary cosmopolitanism and the opportunities for exchanges of learning. One was the invention of printing, and the other some great meetings which brought together people from many parts of Europe on an unprecedented scale.

After the appearance of Gutenberg's Bible in 1456, presses printing with movable type were soon set up in all parts of Europe. By 1490 printing had been introduced into every country of the west; before 1501 as many as 110 different places are claimed to have housed presses, from Stockholm and Lübeck to Toledo, from Budapest and Cracow to Oxford; there was even an abortive effort to introduce printing into Russia. In many places there were large numbers of presses in operation – Venice alone had about 150 in this period. The very rapid diffusion of the actual process of printing (largely due to the enterprise of German craftsmen) is, however, a very different question from that of the effect which it had upon the forms and dissemination of knowledge. In fact it was a long time before printing made its impact as a means of revolutionizing news and knowledge – either new knowledge of recent events or newly appreciated old knowledge.

The advent of the printed word was first appreciated not for the promotion of speed of learning, but for the promotion of certainty of learning. Medieval scholars were dogged by their dependence upon scribes. Whatever the precautions taken – and universities had their own system of inspecting scholarly texts to try to ensure their accuracy – the publication of a work was always liable to involve the multiplication of errors. 'Pray I God that none miswrite thee': Chaucer's prayer at the end of *Troilus and Criseyde* was the prayer of authors at large, and Petrarch, who inveighed against the errors of copyists (as he inveighed against doctors and astrologers), sought to overcome immediate difficulties by employing

49, 50 Guillaume Fichet presenting his *Rhetoric* to Sixtus IV; illumination from a copy printed on vellum prepared for the pope. Right, list of printed books for sale by Peter Schöffer of Mainz in 1470. At the head of the list is the 48-line Bible of 1462, described as a 'beautiful Bible on parchment'

his own copyists, of whom there were three living in his house in 1371, though usually he had as many as five or six. Some mistakes were commoner than others. Leone Battista Alberti in his treatise on architecture – written in the very years that Gutenberg was evolving his movable type – specifically requested future copyists, since in this work the accuracy of numbers was particularly important, always to write the numerals out in full 'for the avoiding of more numerous errors.' For the writer the invention of printing brought the unimaginable delight of being able to approach something like textual finality. It became possible as never before to reproduce large numbers of identical copies. Scholarly accuracy entered a new world. The inventor of printing had performed a divine service, said Polydore Vergil, by saving many Greek and Latin authors from the danger of extinction, and making it possible for 'as much to be printed by one man in one day, as could hardly be written by many in a whole year.' Over twenty years earlier Guillaume Fichet (rector and librarian of the Sorbonne) wrote joyfully to the prior of the university, with whom he was associated in introducing printing to Paris in 1470, about the new opportunity of using print to banish the 'plague' of barbarously copied texts. Fichet himself took steps to print his *Rhetoric*, having discovered that copies of his lectures were circulating in the inaccurate transcriptions of his audiences.

For the first generation the printed book did not differ greatly from manuscripts in appearance, content, and the processes of dissemination. Despite the early adoption by the printers of modern methods of publicizing their works (including book-advertisements, posters, lists, and in 1498 the first printed book catalogue with prices), the problems of access long continued to be the same as they were for manuscripts. Jottings in the notebooks of Leonardo da Vinci, including one for 'Roger Bacon done in print' (though Bacon's works were not printed during the artist's lifetime), are suggestive of the difficulty of tracing texts and of discovering what had appeared in print. Speed and facility in acquiring books still depended on the cultivation of personal contacts, not much different from those which Petrarch, enlisting the English bibliophile Richard

51–53 Printing and scripts. In modelling their types upon contemporary handwriting, printers reflected regional differences. Left top, lines from the Gutenberg Bible whose type was based on northern Gothic script; centre, lines from the manuscript of Cicero's *De Oratore* copied by Poggio Bracciolini in 1428. Poggio was one of the first humanists to develop a new script by imitating Carolingian models (see pp. 185–6), and when about 1465 Sweynheym and Pannartz printed an edition of the *De Oratore*, they adopted the 'antiqua littera' (bottom) in which increasing numbers of books were being written

Bury and the Greek Nicholas Sigeros, had used to enrich the resources of his library in the middle of the fourteenth century. 'A book-printer, of whom I enquired, tells me that he knows of no Greek books having recently appeared,' Dürer wrote home from Venice in 1506 to his humanist friend Willibald Pirckheimer, who pestered the artist from Nuremberg with various bothersome commissions, including requests for books. Even those who, like Pirckheimer, enjoyed easy access to the German book-markets of Frankfurt, Nuremberg and Augsburg, relied upon travels and personal contacts to increase their libraries. Another Nuremberg humanist, the doctor Hieronymus Münzer (1437–1508), collected many of the items for his large library during his studies and travels in different parts, as well as by making special arrangements to have books sent from France and Italy. And although by the time that Münzer was pursuing his studies the art of printing was already old, his student labours still included the lucubrations of the copyist. Two of his volumes (each of about 250 folios) were transcribed by his own hand; one of them, the comedies of Terence, he completed only the year before it first appeared in print. Yet Münzer's library

(which by the time of his death was at least half as large again as that of Cambridge University in 1424) also shows how printing had enlarged the opportunities for book-collecting. And though most early editions were small (on average perhaps about 200 copies) and though the reading public did not become articulate until the sixteenth century, printing also opened new possibilities in painting and music as well as in scholarship. Michelangelo learned from the engravings of Schongauer as did Andrea del Sarto from Dürer's, and Dürer from Mantegna's. Musicians as well as painters could compose for larger circles and extend their influence more widely after the invention of music-printing about 1500.

Given the right contacts and the necessary credit, books might be obtained and circulated as widely and quickly in the days of manuscript as in the early days of printing. The enlarged and emended edition of Livy's *Ab urbe condita*, which was a major achievement of Petrarch's early years (and which continued to exercise a decisive influence upon the textual tradition of Livy down to the *editio princeps* printed at Rome in 1469), had spread rapidly through Italy. When early in 1440 Humphrey duke of Gloucester wrote to

56–60 Above, lines written by Petrarch in the manuscript
of Livy's history which he laboriously pieced together,
corrected and annotated. Above right, Humphrey duke
of Gloucester who played a leading role in the introduction
of humanism into England. A volume of treatises by
St Athanasius, as the autograph inscription in it (opposite
top) records, was translated into Latin for him. Right,
Willibald Pirckheimer, a distinguished Greek scholar, was
the closest friend of Dürer, who made this drawing of him
in 1503. The drawing of the tournament of two cupids (far
right), which appears in the margin of a 1497 Aldine
Aristotle in Pirckheimer's collection, was done either by
Dürer or someone in his studio

Pier Candido Decembrio with requests for various books, he
received the reply that not all the volumes he wanted could be
supplied at once, but even so by July 1441 ducal impatience had been
satisfied by the receipt of at least nine. Vespasiano da Bisticci (1421–
98), the famous Florentine manuscript dealer who advised and supplied many fifteenth-century bibliophiles, engaged forty-five scribes
who wrote two hundred volumes in twenty-two months to meet
the urgent needs of Cosimo de' Medici – a rate of production which
was by no means exceptional. With his contacts in different parts of
Europe Vespasiano was also able to help authors, as he did Zembino
of Pistoia (Sozomen) after the writing of his chronicle. 'When he
had completed it,' Vespasiano recounts, 'he took no steps to have it
copied, but, by my persuasion and encouragement he let it be done
and it quickly attracted so great notice that it was sent to all parts of
Italy, to Catalonia, Spain, France, England and Rome.'

61 The study of Duke Federigo da Montefeltro at Urbino. ▶
Trompe l'œil inlay work shows books from his outstanding collection

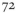

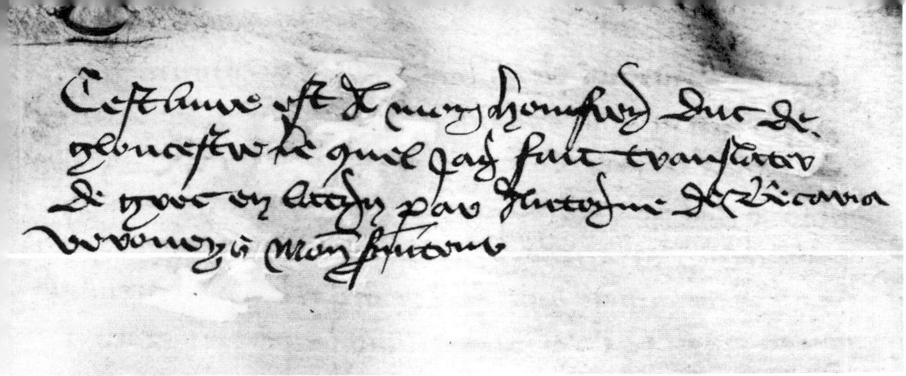
Cest livre est a moy homfrey duc de
glowcestre le quel jay fait translater
de grec en latin par Antoyne de Beccaria
veronoys mon secretaire

While the printers relied on many of the same marketing processes as were used for manuscripts, the works they published perpetuated the same world. A high proportion of the books printed before 1500 were theological, patristic, devotional and religious works of one kind or another, and while the presses of England and Spain from the outset concentrated largely on vernacular writings, about three-quarters of all printed matter surviving from this early period was in Latin. The early printers were commercial, not intellectual adventurers – and even so their presses suffered a high rate of mortality. Gutenberg was far from being the only early printer who failed to make a financial success of his venture. As men of business these itinerant craftsmen did not lead taste; they followed it. And so individuals whose intellectual curiousity marked them out as being ahead of their contemporaries were not necessarily helped by the arrival of printing.

These limitations were evident in the sphere of geographical knowledge. In the fifteenth century most readers' understanding of geography was more likely to be derived from such works as the travels of Marco Polo or 'Sir John Mandeville' – with their rich mixture of fact and fiction – than from any up-to-date account of contemporary explorations. Those who were interested in the facts of discovery would not have found it easy to acquire information. There clearly was such curiosity. The letters which Peter Martyr sent to Italy from October 1494 to 1526 were awaited by correspondents who were 'consumed by desire to be kept regularly informed' of the discoveries he reported direct from Spain. In and after 1493 there were various editions of the letter in which Columbus announced to Ferdinand and Isabella the findings of his first voyage. Little more, however, could have been learnt from this than the fact that certain lands had been discovered to the west which were ostensibly Asiatic and potentially very rich. It was some years before such uncertainties were ended. In 1507 there was published at Vicenza the *Paesi novamente retrovati*, which described the voyages of da Gama and Cabral, and included accounts of Columbus, Cadamosto, Vespucci and Pinzon. The new world was at last laid out to the Renaissance reader – and in French and German as well as

62 The 1507 woodcut world map by Martin Waldseemüller (1470–1518), of which this is a part, was drawn on 12 sheets on a special projection, and is the first map to represent Columbus's discoveries, without ambiguity, as a new continent named America

Italian. It also acquired the recognition of nomenclature. There were various editions of a spurious tract called *Mundus Novus*, based on a letter of Amérigo Vespucci. Finally, in 1507, the geographer Martin Waldseemüller published the accounts of Vespucci's supposed four voyages with the proposal that the new world should be called America. Waldseemüller was himself the first to put the suggestion into action on the large woodcut world map, printed the same year in 1,000 copies, in which he showed North and South America as continents, designated by name.

For all the obstacles and delays which lay between readers and books, the printers had begun by the turn of the fifteenth century to make a notable contribution to the advance of humanist learning. Appropriately enough it was on Italian soil that they first did so. A Latin grammar and Cicero's *De oratore* were the first two books printed in Italy, in 1464–5, and thanks largely to the press of Aldus

Manutius, a continuous series of Greek and Latin classics was produced in large editions from 1495. By the time of Aldus's death in 1515 eighteen major Greek works had been printed, and before 1500 there had been over two hundred editions of Cicero and seventy of Virgil. Humanists, one might think, could hardly complain of a shortage of tools. Yet, outside Italy, they still did so. In the late 1490s Erasmus experienced the difficulties of pursuing Greek researches in Paris, and over ten years after the beginning of the Aldine editions there were still few texts for the study of Greek in the university. In Germany even in the 1520s, though the place of Greek studies had long been recognized, the opportunities for work on it were limited, and both Reuchlin and Melanchthon suffered from textual scarcity when they began lecturing to students. Printing followed humanists more than it made them. The advance was correspondingly slow. Not until 1543 was Greek printed in England.

It took more than the needs of scholarship and learning to demonstrate the possibilities of printing as the means of disseminating new ideas on an unprecedented scale, at an unprecedented rate. It demanded the force of polemic. The theses which Luther pinned up at Wittenberg on 31 October 1517 were said to be known throughout Germany in a fortnight and throughout Europe in a month. In 1520 more than 4,000 copies of one of his works were sold in the space of five days. Printing was recognized as a new power and publicity came into its own. In doing for Luther what the copyists had done for Wycliffe, the printing presses transformed the field of communications and fathered an international revolt. It was a revolution.

In most spheres in the fifteenth century personal contacts proved more fertile than formal connections. Humanist learning was mainly promoted in informal ways. The humanists themselves in fact – in a true Ciceronian spirit – elevated the conversational arts to a new level by the emphasis which they placed upon discursive as well as rhetorical felicity of expression. The pleasurable interchanges of light but polished conversation, as depicted in the court of Urbino by Castiglione, were themselves an accomplishment, an art which could

63 Raphael's *St George and the Dragon* was commissioned as a present for Henry VII of England by Guidobaldo da Montefeltro, duke of Urbino, who in 1504 was appointed to the Order of the Garter

64, 65 Duke Federigo da Montefeltro made Urbino into one of the most cultivated courts of Italy. Luciano Laurana rebuilt his palace, of which the central courtyard (left) achieved the clarity of line aimed at by Piero della Francesca, who worked at Urbino in the 1460s and painted this portrait of the duke (below)

further other arts. By such means (largely intangible), new ways of thinking, like the Neo-Platonism of the Florentine academy or the newly discovered principles of perspective, became household knowledge far away from the places and circles in which they originated. The most important advances of thought (Marx and Freud have demonstrated it for us) always extend far beyond the reading of books.

In the fifteenth century the great ecclesiastical councils promoted the inspiration which derives from the meeting of persons, as well as the meeting of persons with books. The Councils of Constance (1414–18) and of Basel (1431–49), although they were both called for official ecclesiastical purposes, were much more than congregations of leading churchmen. They were unprecedented as ecclesiastical assemblies and surpassed previous church councils, including the celebrated Fourth Lateran Council called by Innocent III in 1215, both in the range of their attendance and in the topics discussed. They might in fact be regarded as a combined form of summit conference, trade fair and ecumenical council, with membership drawn from all parts of Europe, including both secular and ecclesiastical rulers, accompanied and provided for by all the enormous following of retainers, craftsmen and traders who were deemed necessary for the wants of such numbers. Never before had people met together from so many parts on such a scale.

Contemporaries were greatly impressed by the momentousness of such an occasion. 'Here finishes the history of the general council of Constance,' the French diarist Cardinal Guillaume Fillastre ended his lengthy record of the proceedings. 'This council, whose end is now told, was more difficult to assemble than any other general council that preceded it, more strange, surprising, and hazardous in its course, and lasted a longer time.' The exceptional nature of the meeting was itself a stimulus to put facts on record and Ulrich Richental, a citizen of Constance who derived particular pride and pleasure from the commissariat which facilitated it, showed special concern – being fond of numbers – to enumerate all its participants. He ended his account with a full description of 'all the persons who came to the holy council, the lands whence they came and the numbers of their men and horses, as I ascertained them by inquiry from house to house until I collected them all. If I have here forgotten anyone, you must lay it to my ignorance or forgetfulness.' Adding a reminder that not all were present at the same time during the years of the meeting, he then listed a total of 72,460 persons who had come to his city. This vast multitude was composed of all ranks, trades and nations, ranging from 2 popes and 5 patriarchs, the king of the Romans and the representatives of 83 kings of Europe, Asia and Africa, down to 1,700 trumpeters, fifers and musicians, 5,300 priests and scholars, more than 1,400 merchants, innkeepers and tradesmen and 700 prostitutes. The presentation of these numbers alone explains something of the impact of the meeting. The same was true, to a lesser extent, of Basel which, though it began and ended badly, had 500 officially enrolled members by 1434. In

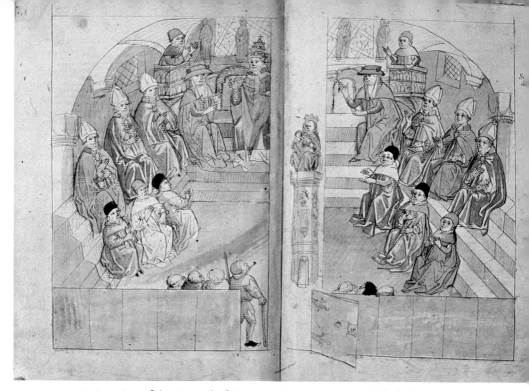

66 A session of the Council of Constance in Constance Cathedral, from a manuscript version of Ulrich Richental's chronicle. Richental was an educated and well-placed layman who received the Emperor-Elect at his house near Constance

addition to the 7 cardinals, 2 patriarchs, 5 archbishops, 43 bishops and 40 abbots who attended it, this council received representatives from 9 kings, and 17 dukes and earls – with all the *mêlée* who accompanied them.

If many people are excited by large crowds, book-lovers are always excited by large collections of books. While Constance and Basel were in sheer size stimulating as international meetings (in the cathedral at Constance people could confess in twelve languages), they also provided a great opportunity for the marketing of ideas and books. Intellectuals (among others) came together from many distant places bringing books with them, and among the important outcomes of the councils was a quickening of the market in all sorts of books. Time hung heavy on the hands of many delegates.

67 Among the various merchants ▶
who provided for the delegates,
were the mobile bakers (opposite),
with ovens on wheelbarrows

The delays in the proceedings at Constance enabled Poggio Bracci-olini (1380–1459) – who then held a post in the papal chancery – to explore the resources of the monastic library at St Gallen, making important finds, including works of Cicero, Quintilian and Lucretius. Others found ample leisure to exchange texts and to acquire copies of already known books. Enormous numbers of scribes were at work at both councils, and the journeys of manuscripts show how distant libraries became enriched (mainly in established fields of Biblical, theological and patristic studies) in Germany, France, Spain, Poland and Sweden.

Among the branches of literature which these exchanges helped to promote, the studies of Italian humanists had a place. It was as the result of meeting Henry Beaufort, bishop of Winchester, at Constance that Poggio was induced to visit England, where his four-year stay (1418–22) marks the first appearance of such an enthusiast. Later councils helped to further these interests. John Wheathampstead, abbot of St Albans, was able to make humanist contacts and probably to increase his library, by his journey to Italy in 1423 to attend the councils of Pavia and Siena. More impor-tant for English humanism was the publicity work by which Zenone da Castiglione, who was sent to Basel as one of the envoys of Henry VI, helped to spread the fame of the duke of Gloucester's patronage. Meanwhile the links forged at Basel by the bishop of Burgos similarly had important results for the extension of the new learning in Spain. And even in Cracow changing fashions of study may have owed something to the Council of Basel.

Finally, in addition to the councils, the century provided another sort of great international assembly. The church jubilee of 1450 was one of a series of such events, started in 1300, but it too proved startling in its proportions. It was the greatest occasion of its kind which there had so far been, and among the attractions which helped to draw enormous throngs of people to Rome was the canonization of the famous Italian preacher, San Bernardino of Siena, who had died only a few years earlier. The crowds which filled the roads through northern Italy were such that contemporaries compared them with ants. They came from all parts. 'One saw innumerable hordes arriving, French, German, Spanish, Portuguese, Greek, Armenian, Dalmatian and Italian, all singing hymns in their own tongue,' recorded a Sienese commentator. The size of this immense concourse was responsible for a serious accident which left a deep impression on many, including the pope. A week before Christmas the milling crowds converging from opposite directions on the bridge of Sant'Angelo produced a vast traffic jam, and in the mob hysteria which broke out nearly two hundred people were crushed or trampled to death. 'Men who had gone through the Turkish wars had seen no more ghastly sight,' wrote an eye-witness. Nicholas V, whose building resources benefited substantially from the jubilee offerings, reconstructed the end of the bridge and had two chapels erected there in memory of the victims.

This jubilee was a memorable occasion. It demonstrated the continuing ecumenical influence of the papacy, the restored authority of the pope after the period of the councils, and the growing attraction of the city of Rome. But it was more. It also revealed, as the crusades had revealed earlier in not dissimilar ways, that the unities of the west were those of the whole of society. The religiosity of the times – which produced other more segmented manifestations of popular fervour – was here on display not only in the grandeur of the papal office but also in the anonymous enthusiasm of the humble.

Yet in emphasizing such exchanges and meeting-points of culture and ideas, it must be remembered that we are considering developments which for the most part affected only a small minority – albeit the most influential minority – of contemporaries. For the vast majority life remained, as it always had been, bounded by horizons which were essentially rural, local and vernacular, punctuated only at intervals, if at all, by the distant events and wider movements which gave some unity to the intellectual currents of the time. As Nicholas of Cusa (1401–64) pointed out, 'such a vast multitude' as comprised the Christian Europe of his time, could not exist without a great deal of misery. 'They live, in many cases, subject to servility and umbrage to those who rule them. As a result, it happens that very few have sufficient leisure to enable them to proceed to a knowledge of themselves' – let alone a knowledge of other people. Europe certainly gained in self-knowledge in the course of the fifteenth century, but the gain was still the gain of a minority. Those who wrote and read books, who transcribed and transported manuscripts, who carried ideas over the frontiers of countries and of languages, and who consulted and conversed in the internationalism of Latin, were a very few, though the all-important few, of the population of Europe. In the traditional threefold division which still aptly described the society of this century, it was those who laboured – the rock of the peasantry upon which society was founded – who vastly outnumbered the remainder who fought and prayed. And although some of the labourers were themselves rising through fighting, praying and reading into a challenging new consciousness, in general they remained, as Cusa said, unknowing because unleisured. Wider knowledge and wider views were the privilege of the chosen.

68 Nicholas of Cusa died at Todi on 11 August 1464, when he was on his way to Ancona to confer with his old friend Pius II, who died three days later. Cusa's last years were mainly spent in papal service in Rome, and this monument to him, erected there in his titular church of San Pietro, shows him with the cardinal's hat which he was given in 1448

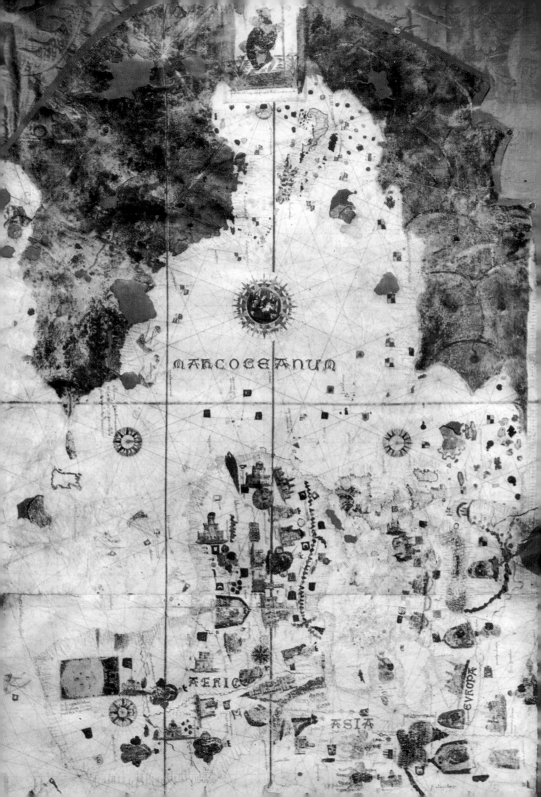

MARCOCEANUM

AFRICA

ASIA

EVROPA

III TRAVELS AND QUESTIONS

The knowledge of past times and of the places on the earth is both ornament and nutriment to the human mind.

LEONARDO DA VINCI

It is extremely rare and unusual for an Indian to offend a Spaniard. PETRARCH (1360)

Much travel will no more make a philosopher than much reading. But the exploration of places, like the exploration of books, can act as a powerful stimulus to the philosophically inclined, and in the fifteenth century increased travel and increased reading were both leading to new questioning. 'The further you go, the more you shall see and know,' as a travel treatise of the period put it. Curiosity breeds criticism and, then as now, travel could help to promote empirical inquiry. 'Taking to the road, I once travelled as a pilgrim to the Holy Sepulchre. And since the more curious is man's wit, the more does he wish to investigate acutely, so I have earnestly set down what I have witnessed on land and sea,' wrote an anonymous fourteenth-century pilgrim. To travel well is to question well and, as both the writing and reading of books (travel-books and others) shows, the fifteenth century became increasingly appreciative of the virtues of the good traveller. More people were undertaking more travel of various sorts, and their explorations, intellectual and geographical, made an important contribution to the outlook of the age.

Among the numerous travellers of the century there were many whose purposes were such that they returned, as they left, more concerned with answers than with questions. Frederick Reiser's heretical missions took him across the length and breadth of Germany before he was finally burned at Strasbourg in 1458. And Peter Payne, who was already well-travelled by the time he joined the Bohemians,

69 Part of the map of Juan de la Cosa, showing Europe and the New World, dated 1500. De la Cosa went with Columbus on his second voyage in 1493, and with Ojeda and Vespucci on their exploration of the South American coast in 1499

went twice to Poland on their behalf, as well as to the Council of Basel, to act as spokesman for the Hussite delegation. Another sort of quest – which in the course of the century brought increasing numbers of students to Italy from north of the Alps – was the search for Greek books and learning. The refugee Byzantine scholar, Janus Lascaris, who had left Constantinople in his youth at the time of its fall, made two journeys back to the east a generation later, in order to collect Greek manuscripts for Lorenzo de' Medici. Guarino da Verona (1374–1460) and Francesco Filelfo (1398–1481), two of the most distinguished humanists of their day, both went to Constantinople specifically to acquire knowledge of Greek. Filelfo, who returned to Venice in 1427 after seven and a half years' residence in the eastern capital, brought back not only many manuscripts but also a Greek wife, Theodora Chrysoloras, niece of Manuel Chrysoloras who from 1397 to 1400 held the newly established chair of Greek in Florence. Another enthusiast for antiquities was Ciriaco d'Ancona (1391–1455) who started travelling when he was nine and who was at Constantinople when it was besieged by Mohammed II. By the time of his death he had spent half a century visiting (often for commercial reasons) different parts of Italy, Greece and Egypt, and left behind six volumes of commentaries recording his investigations of ancient buildings and inscriptions.

71, 72 The arrival of Manuel Chrysoloras (right) in Florence in 1397 marked the real beginning of the continuous study of Greek in Italy. But individuals like Ciriaco d'Ancona, from whose lost drawing of the Parthenon the copy (left) was made, still gained knowledge of the language by visits to Greece

For such men travel was a necessary part of the wider concerns which determined the main course of their lives. Yet professional as well as other journeys might help all sorts of people to widen their intellectual horizons, and the vision of Europe and of things European was certainly promoted in this way. Leonardo da Vinci, who ended his life in France and was as interested in the flow of water in the Black Sea as he was in the nature of the bear-inhabited mountains above Lake Como, wrote with sweeping assurance of the Danube as the 'principal river of Europe as to size.' And Pius II, whose widespread knowledge of his times was matched by his creative literary gifts, had direct experience of Italy and Germany, Bohemia, Burgundy, England and Scotland, which enabled him to write understandingly of the differences between nations, as well as to coin the adjective 'European'. 'Consider,' Nicholas of Cusa admonished his

◀ 70 Detail of northern Germany from a map attributed to Nicholas of Cusa, which became a prototype for early sixteenth-century maps of Europe

readers, 'when you see so many beautiful and various structures of cities, churches, castles and buildings, so many different cloths, so many pictures and decorations, so many languages, so many sciences and arts and books . . .' It was the fertility of the divine intelligence towards which he wanted such considerations directed. But others who were growing, like the cardinal, more noticeably sensitive to visual beauty, often turned their attention towards less strictly spiritual ends.

Even unsophisticated observations of local differences – of costume, taste, behaviour and language – when enlarged and elaborated upon in ways which included art as well as literature, could develop into what we know as a sense of style. Ultimately, this came to involve a developed perception of the dimension of time as well as space. But natural curiosity and the power of observation, even among those who had little to do with humanist history, led in some of the same directions. Pietro Casola, a canon of Milan, was nearing seventy when he set out for Jerusalem in 1494. Even so he was indefatigable in inquiring into everything he saw, and among the things which interested him on arriving in Venice were the fashions of the women. He was fascinated as well as shocked by their low necklines, high heels, and *coiffure*, and reported for certain that much of their hair was false 'because I saw quantities of it on poles, sold by peasants in the Piazza San Marco. Further, I inquired about it, pretending to wish to buy some, although I had a beard both long and white.' Even between Milan and Venice there were many differences, and the work of artists as well as writers gained from the growth of attention to them. 'Her conversation was engaging and in true Greek fashion came pouring out like a torrent. She dressed in the French mode,' wrote Pius II of the young Queen Charlotte of Cyprus, who came to Rome in 1461 to seek papal aid for her kingdom against the Turks. Another queen of Cyprus, who also lost her throne and returned home to Venice in 1489, was painted by Gentile Bellini. This portrait seems to have interested Dürer (who copied it) for its sartorial as well as artistic qualities, and Dürer's own depiction of a Nuremberg housewife beside a Venetian gentlewoman marks a stage in the long evolution of such stylistic consciousness. For all

73 Carpaccio's *Two Venetian Ladies on a Balcony.* ▶
'These Venetian women,' wrote Pietro Casola, 'especially the pretty ones, try as much as possible in public to show their chests – I mean the breasts and shoulders – so much so, that several times when I saw them I marvelled that their clothes did not fall off their backs.'

74 The contrasting styles of the Nuremberg housewife and the Venetian lady pointed out by Dürer.

75 Pisanello's medal of John VIII Paleologus, whose sharply defined features reappeared in some later depictions of eastern emperors

the difference of approach there is a connection – even a progression – between the comment of a German pilgrim that 'a Greek and a Turk are known by their beards,' and Guicciardini's remark that 'if you look closely you will see that from age to age not only do words and men's way of speaking change, but their clothes, building methods, agriculture, and such things.' Although this sense of historical characterization took longer to establish itself, it was assisted by an awareness of regional differences and, since history is as remarkable in resisting time as in moving with it, the two may go together. One of the Florentines who appreciated the appearance of the Greek dignitaries who came to the Council of Ferrara-Florence (1438–9) observed that the attire of the Greeks had not changed since the time of the Apostles.

The pilgrim literature of the fifteenth century is particularly illuminating of the ways in which travel could affect thought. Pilgrimages played an important part in late medieval religious practice. Jerusalem, Rome, St James of Compostella and other less famous (and less recognized) shrines attracted increasing numbers of pilgrims, and the variety of surviving pilgrim books are among the evidence which attests the popularity of such journeys. Writings related to the traffic of the pilgrim routes were already considerable in quantity before this period, but the works of this kind which were written in the fifteenth century, although in part both traditional and repetitive, were distinctive as well as numerous. The demands of growing numbers of literate pilgrims produced various guide-books of the kind familiar to modern travellers, some of them composed by laymen who were anxious to provide for the needs of others like themselves. By the beginning of the sixteenth century intending visitors to the Holy Land could equip themselves with handy compendia of information about the customs and beliefs of Muslims and the sects of the eastern church, and introductions to the alphabets of Greeks, Arabs, Armenians or Jews; they might also have access to phrase-books in different languages which included such items as 'How much?' or 'Give me that.' The German noble, Arnold von Harff, gave the intending pilgrim the following assistance for finding accommodation in Greece.

> Woman, shall I marry you?
> Where shall I sleep?
> Good woman, let me sleep with you.
> Where is the inn?
> Woman, I am already in your bed.

Perhaps it is hardly surprising that many critics as various as Thomas à Kempis and the English Lollard, William Thorpe, objected to the practice of pilgrimage as an abused form of secular entertainment. What is more revealing is to see that pilgrims might themselves be provoked by their pilgrimages into criticism of ecclesiastical abuses. Some of the very people whom one might have expected to be most conservative in their acceptance of devotional practices, returned home in a questing, questioning mood.

Felix Faber was unusual in that he made a double journey from Ulm to the Holy Land in the space of a few years. It is evident from the long account which he wrote of these travels that he was a devout but not a credulous man, and he was conscious that such expeditions were a way of advancing in theological as well as personal knowledge. 'I say of a truth, that in forty weeks of this pilgrimage a man learns to know himself better than in forty years elsewhere,' he wrote. A pilgrimage was a recognized voyage of self-discovery, the pilgrimage to Jerusalem the epitome of life itself. But, in addition, it could help the understanding of theology – among laymen as among clerks – as Faber himself vividly realized when on his pilgrim galley he saw for the first time people clapping their hands for joy, and was reminded of the words of the 46th Psalm, 'O clap your hands, all ye people.' Such experience was valuable, he thought.

> We see with our own eyes at the present day that mere laymen, with no knowledge of the Holy Scriptures, after they have made a pilgrimage to the holy places and have returned from thence, argue about the Gospel and the prophets, talk upon theological subjects, and sometimes overcome and set right learned divines in their interpretation of difficult passages of Holy Scripture, because no Catholic returns from thence without having become more learned.

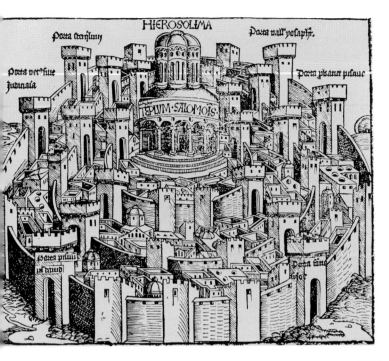

76–78 Pilgrims setting out for the Holy Land (below right, from a guide book), or returning from Compostella (below left), traditionally went, like the Apostles, barefoot, staff in hand; but countless pilgrims reached Jerusalem (left, a schematic view) on the galleys which sailed regularly from Venice to the Holy Land

93

Pilgrimages certainly occasioned a great deal of talk and some pilgrims, Felix Faber included, were not inhibited about recording doubts which it raised. The ways in which they approached places and objects of veneration, and the ways in which they discussed and described them afterwards, illustrate the growth of empirical attitudes and the increasing confidence of both laity and clergy in making personal decisions as to what could justifiably be doubted. Significant among such doubts were those about relics.

The visiting of relics was an accepted and important part of a pilgrim's devotions, and relic-collecting, like pilgrimaging, loomed large in fifteenth-century religion. Among the celebrated royal collections of the time was that of Louis XI, who sent to Florence on his deathbed to ask for the loan of the miraculous ring of St Zenobius, the city's patron saint. Much artistic effort as well as much devotion was inspired by relics in the later Middle Ages. Lorenzo Ghiberti (1378–1455) interrupted his work on the bronze doors of the Florentine baptistery in the 1430s in order to design a new shrine for the relics of St Zenobius, and in the following decade another Florentine artist endangered his career by getting involved in an attempt to steal a reliquary from a church in Rome. The great value which was set upon relics produced some of the most gorgeous ceremonial of the century, as well as robbery in high places. The solemnities arranged by Martin V and Pius II for the enshrining respectively of the body of St Monica and the head of St Andrew were among the greatest occasions of their pontificates. Pius II clearly felt that the peak of his reign had been reached when the head of the Apostle was placed beside the bones of St Peter and St Paul in a tremendous Holy Week ceremony in 1462. The papal tears, the unwonted pedestrian passage of the cardinals through the muddy streets of Rome, the blazing lights and the distinguished visitors and enormous crowds, all emphasized the magnitude of the occasion. It was a splendid opportunity for rhetorical publicity against the Turks – as well as for public weeping.

By the end of the Middle Ages the ancient practice of relic-collecting had made only too conspicuous the danger which had already been foreseen in the thirteenth century; saints and relics

79–81 The respect for relics. Pius II was buried in the chapel of St Andrew, in old St Peter's, Rome, 'in the place where he had enshrined the head of St Andrew the Apostle'. The relief below shows him receiving the reliquary. Innocent VIII is represented on his funeral monument (above left), holding the tip of the Holy Lance sent to him by Bajezid II. One end of Ghiberti's new shrine for St Zenobius (above right) shows the saint reviving a boy crushed by an ox-cart

had multiplied to such an extent that they hindered as well as helped devotion. Contributing to the centuries-old proliferation caused by the competitive rivalry of collectors was the arrival of eastern relics as a result of Turkish conquests. St Andrew's head, brought to Italy in 1461 by Thomas Paleologus from Patras when he was driven out of the Morea, was one such acquisition. Another, which came to Innocent VIII (1484–92) at the end of his pontificate, as a valued bribe of Turkish diplomacy, was a fragment of the Holy Lance which had been lost to Christendom with the fall of Constantinople. Such gains – for all their worth – could be a source of considerable embarrassment. In the 1460s Pius II and Cardinal Bessarion were concerned with a long lawsuit which arose over rival claims to the body of St Luke. The long-established claim of the Benedictines of Padua to this possession was contested after the Turkish occupation of Bosnia, when some Franciscans arrived in Venice with what also purported to be the body of the saint. The case was complicated by the fact that the Vatican had a head of St Luke. The Benedictines, whose relic was headless, made play with the fact that the saint was unlikely to have had two heads, but the Franciscans (whose imported body was entire) were nevertheless victorious. Even after this, however, an arm of St Luke as well as the Vatican head continued to be displayed in Rome.

It was one of the hazards of late medieval pilgrimage that the more conscientious the pilgrim, the more likely he was to discover such disturbing anomalies. 'All respectable pilgrims to Jerusalem . . . at whatever towns they stop on the way, they straightway make inquiries about the churches and the relics of the saints, and visit them.' The greater the thoroughness in such devotions, the greater the demands upon the credulity – if not the faith – of the worshipper, and Felix Faber, who carefully followed his own directive, was not alone in experiencing some disillusion as a result. He saw collectors and exploiters of collectors in action, and was disgusted. On his second pilgrimage in 1484, he visited the cave near Bethlehem where the massacre of the Holy Innocents was supposed to have taken place. A member of the party who was a wealthy noble (and for some reason, as Faber noted, such men were specially

◀ 82 Carpaccio's *Miracle of the Relic of the True Cross* shows a man possessed by devils being healed by the relic, which belonged to a Venetian community. The large numbers of boats in Venice astonished visitors such as Philip de Comines, who calculated there must be about 30,000

interested in this kind of relics) approached their Muslim guide, since he had failed to excavate any bones on the site, with a view to purchasing 'an entire body' of one of the Innocents. He was told that there was a monopoly in such exports, and that he would have to apply to the sultan at Cairo. Faber, finding this arrangement 'insulting, tricky and unjust', made his own inquiries and discovered that stillborn babies were regularly prepared by wounding and embalming for sales to such unsuspecting Christian princes. He was not afraid to draw the moral. 'Thus are Christ's faithful people mocked and robbed of their money, for these infidels know our ardent desire for the possession of relics, and therefore set out for sale wood said to be part of the Holy Cross, and nails, and thorns and bones, and many other things of the same kind, to delude the unwary and cheat them out of their money. I do not set much value upon new relics brought from parts beyond the sea, especially those which have been purchased from Saracens or from Eastern Christians.' The same expedition also enabled this observant pilgrim to resolve his doubts about the nature of the 'Virgin's milk', which was displayed as a relic in many parts of Europe, and which had already been publicly castigated by San Bernardino, who declared that 'All the buffalo cows of Lombardy would not have as much milk as is shown about the world' as the Virgin's. Faber likewise doubted but he demanded positive proof, and was satisfied that he had found it when he 'learned by experience' in a grotto at Bethlehem that such 'milk' was 'nothing more than moisture which drops from a rock.'

While pilgrimage could in some cases resolve existing doubts, in others it prompted new ones. Some of the most enthusiastic pilgrims were also the most critical, and were finding themselves – long before Erasmus – forced into scepticism at ecclesiastical shrines. In the later 1430s Pero Tafur spent several years travelling in Europe and the Middle East, including a visit to the Holy Land. He was a good Christian but he was also an empirical traveller, with a passionate desire to go everywhere and to see everything. (He took advantage of being shipwrecked in the Aegean to explore the ruins of Troy.) Like others who enlarge their horizons by asking many questions Tafur had his own criteria for judging the answers. Some doubts, he was well aware, were more legitimate than others, but his own faith was hedged with scepticism and he did not temper his questioning with tact. When he arrived in Nuremberg after his visit to the east, Tafur went with some celebrated ecclesiastics who were then meeting there, to be shown the relics alleged to have been brought by Charlemagne from Jerusalem. Among them was the steel lance which, the visitors were told, had pierced Christ's side. 'But', Tafur records, 'I said that I had seen the real one in Constantinople, and I believe that if the great people had not been with me, I should have been in peril from the Germans for what I said.'

Criticism of relics and miraculous objects could mean impugning the faith of the clergy no less than that of credulous believers. Both could be dangerous as well as undesirable undertakings. Another youthful pilgrim, whose attitude resembled that of Tafur, shows how easily worries about relics could turn into questioning of the church. Arnold von Harff was still less than thirty when he returned home to Germany in the last months of 1499 after a three-year pilgrimage which had taken him to Rome, the Holy Land and Compostella. His devotion and thoroughness are abundantly demonstrated by the catalogues of holy relics which he earnestly listed in all the places he visited. All the more illuminating, therefore, is the young man's scarcely veiled disdain for what, with delicate irony, he chose to call clerical confusions on so important a matter. On his extensive travels he was constantly bothered by the hagiographical duplications he encountered. Arms of St Thomas were displayed in Rome, Rhodes and India; the head of St James the Less was to be seen in Venice and at Compostella; the body of St Dominic was shown to him at Bologna in Italy and at Santo Domingo de la Calzada in Castile. It was indeed a trial for the faith of the faithful. Von Harff clearly found it so and his reactions are indicative. For him, as for so many others, relics remained 'very honourable' objects of devotion; he was tireless in seeking them out and in enumerating them for the benefit of other travellers. What was unworthy, and what he did not hesitate to call in question, was the good faith of the clergy for, as he saw it, it was their rivalry and fraudulence which had allowed and perpetuated these deceptions.

'The confusions of the clergy I leave to God to settle,' he remarked with obvious insinuation on several occasions. His description of what happened to him at Compostella says much for contemporary attitudes – both of churchmen and of pilgrims.

> Item it is claimed that the body of St James, the greater apostle, rests or lies in the high altar, others say in truth no, that he lies in Toulouse in Languedoc. . . . I desired, with great presents, that they should show me the holy body. They replied that anyone who did not believe truly that the holy body of St James, the greater apostle, lay in the high altar, but doubted and therefore desired to see the body, he would immediately become mad like a mad dog. From this I had learnt all I wanted to know . . .

Doubt and devotion are no more irreconcilable than criticism of the church and loyalty to Christ. But the attitudes of the devout were changing, and in some cases faster than the church was able to adjust to them. 'Nature', said Leonardo da Vinci, 'revenges on those who wish to work miracles.' Sixteenth-century reformers inflicted their own retribution – in ways which to them seemed natural enough – on the many shrines and wonder-working centres of the Middle Ages which had so long attracted the attention of critics and reformers. Previous failure to deal with such abuses was partly the result of the strenuous particularism of the late medieval church. Local cults, like private devotions, easily grew distorted, as the central authorities of the church readily admitted, though they might not be capable of putting through the necessary correction. The cult of the bleeding host of Wilsnack in Brandenburg, which became established and won great renown as the result of a reported miracle in the 1380s, was the subject of a considerable number of official inquiries in the fifteenth century. Those who became involved in them included John Hus, Stanislaus of Znaim and Nicholas of Cusa, but despite the unanimity of condemnation all efforts at suppression failed until the middle of the sixteenth century. The borderline between genuine devotion and fraudulent exploitation was often hard to determine, but the inability of ecclesiastical authorities, from popes, cardinal-legates and councils downwards, to exercise control encouraged the growth of spontaneous questioning.

At the same time that certain individuals were formulating questions as the result of extensive geographical travels, others were arriving at some of the same points through the study of books. New readers reading old books and old readers reading and writing new ones came to some parallel conclusions, even when they belonged to such different worlds as those of Italian humanists and English heretics. While acute observers were capable, through native intelligence, of deciding that 'what can be done by natural causes ought not to be ascribed to miracles,' those whose studies were leading to fuller understanding of historical processes came to see that what was appropriate for Christianity in the first century might not be suitable for the fifteenth. Coluccio Salutati combined respect for Biblical authority with scepticism about the reported miracles of recent periods. To go to Aachen or Rome expecting special effects from relics or hoping for miracles was a form of self-deception, said the Hussite bishop John Rokycana, who was among the people who associated the search for the miraculous with a lack of true faith. Pietro Pomponazzi (1462–1525), who thought that all miraculous events ought to be explicable by natural causes, considered that belief in miracles belonged to particular stages of religious development, and Christianity – since it was a historical religion, subject like any other to growth and decay – had passed the phase at which such occurrences could take place. It might in fact (it was coming to be seen) be wholly legitimate to question in the present a happening of a kind which must be implicitly accepted in circumstances of the past. 'I find it easy to believe that in every age many things have been regarded as miracles, which were nothing of the sort,' wrote Guicciardini, who was nonetheless ready to accept that they were signs of God's grace. By other channels, associated with scriptural reading and Biblical fundamentalism, other contemporaries were challenging the belief in the miraculous. Obscure English Lollards, like Bohemian reformers, attacked the veneration of images and relics, seeing them as ecclesiastical frauds and arguing that pilgrims would do better to give alms to the poor.

This century produced a considerable number of new readers and of new – or newly discovered – books. It was an age in which more people, of a great variety, were becoming appreciative of the value of literacy and the power of the written word, and printing arrived to meet an existing need as well as to stimulate these trends still further. Literate laymen were becoming commoner and they included, in addition to well-placed nobility and gentry, tradespeople and apprentices who attained varying degrees of ability to read and write. Throughout the Middle Ages literacy included a large number of different stages, even among those who never aspired to Latin learning. People who could read might never learn to write, and some of the new authors included persons who could do neither. St Catherine of Siena (c. 1347–80), whose ability to read was reported to have been miraculously promoted, left behind a considerable correspondence in addition to her *Dialogue*, but probably never learnt to write and to the end dictated to a member of her household. The Englishwoman Margery Kempe, whose posthumous celebrity rests upon the fact that she decided in 1436 to turn her religious experiences into a book, provides an interesting example of book-consciousness among the pious laity since, as she put it, she 'hungered right sorely after' holy reading, but both her reading and her writing had to be done with the help of others. Another similar case is that of Johann Schiltberger, who returned home to Bavaria in 1427 having spent about thirty years in different sorts of captivity in the east. At the age of sixteen he was made prisoner after the defeat at Nicopolis, where he narrowly escaped the sentence of execution he had seen inflicted on many of his companions. Schiltberger, like Margery Kempe, was influenced by the world of books. He too, probably in the same way dictating the record of a remarkable life, was in touch with the concerns of the literate and observed the difference between the laity of Armenia who dared not read the Gospels and 'our own learned laity . . . who, when they come across a book, read what they find in it.'

The advance of lay reading did not depend upon printing but was certainly helped by it. And, while the various categories of religious works were in general the most numerous, in various parts of Europe

83, 84 Sebastian Brant (right), whose *Narrenschiff* (1494) appeared early in various languages besides German, was a firm believer in vernacular religious reading for laymen. Left, a page from the first vernacular Bible to be printed in Bohemia in 1489, showing St Matthew writing his Gospel

(with the exception of England) vernacular Bibles found a market, particularly in Germany and Italy. It was not only ill-educated clergy who were hungry for meaty religious reading. Savonarola, who produced a simplified Italian version of his *Triumph of the Cross* for the benefit of those who could not read Latin, and who wanted his profession of faith to be available to the ignorant as well as the learned, remarked in that work that what most riveted the attention of his audiences was the exposition of scripture. 'The reading, hearing, and study of Holy Scripture', he said, 'is both a cause of our Christian life and the substance and foundation of our religion.' Though Erasmus's advocacy of Biblical familiarity for weavers at the shuttle and ploughmen at the plough has justly become famous, such persons were already practising what he preached well before his time. If you believe in God, Erasmus said to the layman addressed in the *Enchiridion*, you must believe 'nothing is so certain and unquestionable

103

as that which you read in the scriptures.' In England for more than a century, humble followers of Wycliffe had, with varying degrees of aberration and fidelity, been continuing through underground Bible studies the tradition inspired by his teaching. Reading and religion went together for many different people. 'For the knowledge of God comes of diligence of reading . . . Truly if not all men reading know God, how shall he know that reads not?' It was an early follower of Wycliffe who asked that question, but whereas in England the reading of the vernacular Bible – and other texts – became a leading criterion for judging the heresy of book-running artisans, there were plenty of orthodox across the whole of Europe who, as time went on, would have found little to quarrel with in such a proposition.

Yet Bible reading by the self-educated or semi-literate could prompt strange questions and conclusions. It clearly did so in England where Lollards were accused of asserting or disputing such points as 'the Blessed Sacrament of the altar is a great devil of hell and a synagogue' or 'the earth is above the sky'. Theology is never a safe subject, least of all when treated by weavers. But the readers went on reading, and the declaimers went on declaiming.

> Some think they are so very shrewd
> That sense enough they have indued
> That now by all their subtle wit
> They can interpret Holy Writ,

wrote Sebastian Brant when Luther was eleven. His apocalyptic vision of the coming end of the church fitted into a long tradition, but events were soon to add force to the words of his satire. The Bible has acted as an armoury for all sorts of militant endeavours, and it was not only in Germany that peasant risings turned to it for textual justification. As Brant remarked, 'The peasants now attain the fore,/And scholars hide behind the door.' Not all scholars were in retreat, but the fifteenth century certainly demonstrated the dangers of artisans' literacy. Events justified the church's view that their reading needed to be controlled. And in England, where such controls were particularly in evidence, a bishop lost office for trying to answer heretics in their own coinage, by refuting their unorthodox conclusions in theological works written for their benefit in the vernacular. Reginald Pecock, bishop of Chichester, advocated in his *Repressor of Over Much Blaming of the Clergy* (itself an attempt to put the advice into practice) that the most effective way of stopping the common people reproving the clergy would be to give them better means of understanding; in particular 'much good would come forth if a short compendious logic were devised for all the common people in their mother tongue.' Pecock's temerity cost him his see in 1457. His books were burnt and he ended his days in monastic confinement.

The travels of the later Middle Ages took people, bodily and mentally, beyond the bounds of Christendom and here, too, new worlds were being opened by exploration. The pagan past as well as the non-Christian present could be viewed more dispassionately the better it was known, and knowledge of both had been very considerably extended before the fifteenth century came to an end. Old ideas of the incompatible, irreconcilable aspects of ancient, Muslim, and Christian beliefs went on, but new ones, significant for the future, were appearing beside them.

The idea of the crusade, which had so long dominated Christian thinking about the east, continued to be advocated and pursued. By no means all the gestures made on its behalf – even the most elaborately symbolic ones of late medieval chivalry – were purely formal, though the ineffectiveness of a number of them fostered a certain disillusion. Philip the Good, duke of Burgundy, who was born in the same year that his father was captured at Nicopolis, went on proclaiming his desire to campaign against the Turks well into the 1460s, by which time his own age made it, to say the least, unlikely. But there is no reason to doubt the sincerity of his enthusiasm, which impressed contemporaries as much as that of Pope Pius II. The Spanish reconquest of Muslim territory, persistently pursued by Ferdinand and Isabella, and triumphantly completed with their entry into Granada in 1492, to some extent offset the failures and disillusionments of the east. And at the end of the century, as at the beginning, there were still idealistic monarchs who thought and talked in terms of an eastern crusade. 'I wish that my kingdom lay upon the confines of Turkey,' Richard III of England (1483-5) is reported to have declared. 'With my own people alone and without the help of other princes I should like to drive away not only the Turks, but all my foes.' Yet even for those who were not situated at such a safe distance, these conventional ideas became more and more like expressions of wishful thinking as time went on.

In the fourteenth century and even earlier, there were signs of the emergence of a new attitude. Better understanding of the east as well as the growing sense of insecurity in the west caused the problem of the Turks to be considered from pacific points of view. Two worlds, even when mutually estranged, cannot co-exist for generations without some adjustments of mental approach, and critics of papal policies had long found reasons for objecting to the whole idea of the crusade. Already before the days of Gower and Langland and Boccaccio more people were becoming prepared to admit the merits of Muslims, to point out the similarities as well as the basic discrepancies between the teachings of Christ and Mohammed, and to suggest the advantages of expanding agreement before acting upon disagreement, using missionary rather than military methods. It took time, of course, as it usually does, for changes of opinion to receive official recognition. As late as 1541 there were fears of the dangers of printing the Koran and it was long before the Turks gained equal diplomatic standing among the western European powers. But the field of tolerance was growing, and individuals illustrate the ways of its growth.

Travel-books and the inquiries of travellers contributed to this change of view. As the pressure of the Turks upon eastern Europe increased, so did the body of observed fact and descriptive literature which was available in the west about the nature of Islam. Although much of this travel and writing was primarily concerned with dis-cussions and pleas for crusading objectives, new notes become detectable beside old prejudices. Some of the travel literature which circulated in manuscript or was printed during the last part of the fifteenth century gave fairly full accounts of Muslim beliefs. Schiltberger (whose work seems to have been popular and went through several early editions) was well qualified to give such an account and his description of Mohammedanism, though ingenuous, was more open-minded, as well as more knowledgeable, than that of many others. Von Harff – who visited Cairo in a very different manner – also thought fit to describe Muslim beliefs and sects, and was impressed by their devotion and optimistic of the possibilities of peaceful conversion. 'I believe, in truth, that if one could preach in this land the people would soon be converted, since they are very credulous.' Even that most imaginative and popular of medieval travel-books, 'Sir John Mandeville', included a narrative of Mohammed and the Koran which was more tolerant than totally misleading. The Saracens, it said, 'grant well that all the works of Christ and all his words and his teachings and his Evangels are good and true, and his miracles true and clear; and that the Virgin Mary was a good maiden and a holy before the birth of Christ and after also, and undefiled; and that those that believe perfectly in God shall be safe. And for as much as they go thus near our faith in these points and many other, methink that much the quicker and the lightlier they should be converted to our law through preaching and teaching of Christian men.'

Individuals who had direct experience of Islam went out of their way, even when arguing the case for conquest, to point out the humanity and virtues of Muslims. In the 1420s a native of Crete called Emmanuel Piloti, who had resided for more than thirty-five years in Mohammedan lands, wrote a work (which was translated twenty years later for the benefit of Eugenius IV) advocating the recovery of the Holy Land by way of Cairo and Alexandria. The idea was not original but it is significant that despite his militant project and conventional hostility to Islam (*foy bestiale*, he repeatedly calls it), Piloti pleaded that the Saracens were good people who should be treated honourably and courteously. And, since Muslims and Christians for all their differences were alike in professing one God, he proposed that ten masters from each side should meet to examine, consider and determine the true faith which 'every creature of the whole world' should 'believe and obey to the end of the world.' It was a far-sighted suggestion which others were to take further.

85, 86 Gentile Bellini was sent in 1479 as official envoy from Venice to Constantinople where he painted this portrait of a Turkish artist in imitation of an Islamic miniature. Opportunity for such interchanges continued throughout the century in Spain where Muslims' rights were recognized till 1502; the relief at right shows the forcible baptism of the Moors of Granada

Philip the Good sent two emissaries to the east in order to forward his crusading project. One of these was Bertrandon de la Broquière, an enterprising and observant squire of Guienne, who learnt a great deal during his journeyings between 1432 and 1433, which took him through much Turkish territory, for after a pilgrimage to Jerusalem and Mount Sinai he returned home overland, visiting both Constantinople and Adrianople. The account which he wrote up for the benefit of the duke contained a considerable amount of information about Muslims and their way of life, which owed much to the author's native curiosity, as well as to the nature of his commission. 'As I was incessantly hearing Mohammed spoken of, I wished to know something about him.' In addition to the military data which he collected, de la Broquière asked many questions about Mohammed, his place of burial and the pilgrimage to Mecca. He also managed to obtain from the chaplain attached to the Venetian consul at Damascus a Latin life of the prophet and a copy of the Koran, which he presented to the duke of Burgundy on his return and which later helped the writings of Jean Germain, bishop of Chalon-sur-Saône. De la Broquière specifically pointed out to his readers the kindnesses he had received at the hands of non-Christians. He owed his life on several occasions to the services of his Mameluke

companion, who dissuaded two of his would-be assassins with the argument that 'after all, God had created the Christians as well as the Saracens.' De la Broquière himself was not far from putting the converse case. The Turks, he said, were 'men of probity, and charitable towards each other.'

It is indicative of the ways in which increasing traffic had enlarged the body of tolerant opinion that Jean Germain, who was commissioned in 1450 by the duke of Burgundy to write to enlist French help in a crusade, drew attention to the influence of trade and travel as causes of contemporary *nonchaloir*. 'By reason of voyages on wars, trade and pilgrimage made by people of all estates, nobles and others, in regions of the east . . . many people', he said, 'seeing the great lordships, towns and peoples in great number under the obedience of Mohammed, often return full of scruples.' Germain, viewing such intercourse from the traditional viewpoint of his master, thought that the best answer to such corrupting indifference was the revival of the holy war. He was essentially a representative of the old school. But some other intellectuals at this time, with whom he was in correspondence, and who had pondered deeply on the problem of the east, arrived at very different conclusions which themselves reflected the growing tolerance of those eastern travellers whose influence the bishop of Chalon so much suspected. Nicholas of Cusa and John of Segovia were both against military aggression and concerned to find grounds of agreement with Islam; both thought in terms of some kind of conference to attain it; and both worked upon the text of the Koran as the essential preliminary to such approaches. And Cusa actually suggested that a foregathering of merchants would be a helpful method of collecting first-hand information about Islam.

'We are bound to believe', wrote Nicholas of Cusa, 'that ignorance is the cause of error and evil.' Working on this assumption in 1460 he 'sieved' through the doctrine of Islam in the book of its faith in order to show 'the truth of the Gospel out of the Koran.' He was concerned, that is, in a work of textual exploration, to demonstrate that behind the discrepancies and differences lay a basis of belief common to the Koran and the Gospels. It had to be admitted that in denying Christ's divinity and resurrection the Koran denied the true nature of Christ and fundamental Christian belief; Mohammed himself was a man of the world, manifestly not comparable to the prophets; the Koran was a work of Arab poetry, erroneous, inconsistent, far from divine. But Muslims admitted the testimony of the prophets, the Virgin Birth and the prophetic power of Christ. The very principles of the Koran were derived essentially from the light of the Gospel and, rightly interpreted, did not contradict the doctrine of the Trinity. On Cusa's demonstration the Koran could itself be used to show the superiority of Christ and the Gospel over Mohammed and his book, and in a way which could only with conspicuous inconsistency deny the divinity of Christ. Islam could in fact be convicted out of its own mouth; its own faith was a witness to the Gospel.

Before this, John of Segovia, a Spanish ecclesiastic who was both friend and correspondent of Cusa, had completed by the time of his death in 1458 a new translation of the Koran. The fall of Constantinople had played a part in stimulating this work which involved him, as he describes, in considerable labours, both in obtaining a good text and in having it translated from the Arabic. Segovia was convinced – in true humanist fashion – that accurate textual studies must precede efforts to convert Muslims. He shared Cusa's view that a proper examination of the Koran was the primary necessity.

He also (perhaps more importantly) revealed a true humanist's instinct in seeing that it was no good talking down to those you wished to convert; they must be approached on a level of equal understanding. The equality of the conference table should replace the inequality of the sermon.

In the original mind of Nicholas of Cusa these ideas found a distinctive form. It was an expression of the new outlook which was percolating through his time – as well as of his own originality – that in the months of alarm which followed the news of the fall of Constantinople Cusa wrote a treatise, *De Pace Fidei*, which aimed to discover 'how lasting peace based on agreement and truthful means might be established', and envisaged doing so by a conference of wise men of different nations and religions assembled at Jerusalem. In the visionary form into which he cast his conviction Cusa conceived of peace being secured by general acceptance of 'one orthodox faith', the common denominator of which he was at pains to define. 'If everyone loves wisdom, do they not presuppose the same wisdom?' On this premise it was possible to envisage that 'all would recognize that there is, in spite of many varieties of rites, but one religion.' It was an idealistic dream, not a proposal of practical politics. Yet it accords with the aim of discovering the roots of ultimate agreement which guided the sieving of the Koran. And Nicholas of Cusa, for all the isolation of his mystical aspirations, struck a note which could arouse sympathetic echoes in many of his contemporaries: the sense, that is, that spiritual convictions transcended rites and ceremonies, and that the bounds of belief were determined by personal and spiritual rather than by ecclesiastical horizons.

Such ideas went much further in the end than the problem of relations between Muslim east and Christian west. They could be used to embrace the differences inside as well as beyond the Christian world, to discover a way of harmonizing the present divergences of Christendom or the discrepancies of belief between past and present. At the end of the century the leading objective of the Florentine Academy was the creation of a philosophical synthesis to reconcile Christianity and Platonism and embrace all religious experience.

Marsilio Ficino (1433–99) and his short-lived follower, Pico della Mirandola (1463–94), carried further Cusa's belief that 'Holy Scripture and the philosophers have said the same thing in different terms.' They approached an old problem in a new way. Their syncretism stemmed from the conviction that religious experience belongs to the very nature of human existence and that the individual's sense of the divine is common to all religions. 'Divine worship is as natural for men almost as neighing is for horses or barking for dogs,' said Ficino. 'When I say religion, I mean the instinct common and natural, to all peoples, by which a Providence is always conceived and worshipped everywhere as queen of the world.' The task of definition was essentially one of philosophical comprehension though it also retained an essentially theological cast. Ficino's attempts to define the community of religion in Platonic, Neo-Platonic and Christian philosophy, were his *Theologia Platonica* and *De Christiana Religione*. The intellectual brilliance of Pico della Mirandola took him to Greek, Hebrew and Arab sources – ranging, as he put it, 'throughout all the masters of philosophy, pledged to the tenets of none' – in the aim of discovering a universal spiritual harmony, reducing the diversity of philosophies to a single mystical truth. It was an aim of awe-inspiring grandeur, the concept of a genius more than the product of an age. Yet the lives of both Mirandola and Ficino reflected the uncertainties of their time as well as rising above them. Ficino ended his life as a canon of Florence. Mirandola responded to the call of Savonarola and had resolved before his death to give away his possessions and follow the preacher's example.

87 Pico della Mirandola, who was only 31 when he died in 1494, became famous in 1486 when the papacy banned thirteen of the 900 theses, drawn from many sources, which he had declared himself ready to defend in public disputation at Rome. The ban was not lifted until 1493, despite the efforts of his protector, Lorenzo de' Medici

88, 89 Marsilio Ficino's primary concern is strikingly illustrated by this medal, the obverse of which shows him near the end of his life; he had studied all the available sources of Platonic and Neo-Platonic doctrine. The members of the Florentine 'academy' which centred on him called him 'another Plato'

In various different contexts in the fifteenth century there appeared a similar belief in the power of words and argument, a sense that rifts and animosities might be healed by discussion. For all the differences, there was a similarity of conviction behind the misguided suggestions of Bishop Pecock, the negotiations by which the Council of Basel tried to settle the divisions between the Hussites and the church, and the meeting of the Roman church with the Greeks at the Council of Ferrara-Florence to thrash out the long-standing points of theological divergence between the western and eastern churches. In every case the attempt failed. Pecock was disgraced; the conciliar compromise with the Hussites was rejected by later popes; the settlement with the Greeks was short-lived. Yet the efforts are themselves highly significant of contemporary frames of mind.

The fifteenth century was a time when words were coming into their own. They could not replace swords but their use as tools was growing, and moving further into the field of politics and public events. The expansion of education, the passion for definition and rationalization and for improving intellectual procedures, the increasing appreciation and currency of the written – as well as the expertly spoken – word, all helped to place a greater premium upon public disputation. Western diplomacy was born in a society which was learning to talk and to write in new ways. And though war was far from being displaced, even pacifism was beginning to become more possible. The appreciation of peace as such was alien to the chivalric temperament of the Middle Ages, but by the fifteenth century individuals were arguing the cause of peace in the west for its own sake, not simply as the necessary preliminary to eastern aggression. The pacifists of the century included not only outstanding unorthodox thinkers such as the Bohemian Peter Chelčicky – whose radicalism was of the heretical Biblical variety – but leading states-men such as George of Poděbrady, who produced an ambitious plan (which remained a paper proposal) for an international assembly to settle the differences and secure the peace of Europe. That great diplomatic development of the century, the international conference, was adapted in practice as well as advocated in theory for the express purpose of settling disputes which otherwise belonged ex-clusively to the forum of war. The Congress of Arras in 1435 represented an attempt to argue out Anglo-French discords of the Hundred Years' War. Here as elsewhere, what was hoped for did not correspond with what was done. But things which fail may affect events, and thoughts about events, as much as things which succeed.

'There is henceforth nothing', wrote Pius II with misplaced optimism, shortly before his death in 1464, 'to prevent Pope Pius from going on the crusade against the Turks and many advantages may result. Confident in this hope he is girding himself for this enterprise and preparing for the greatest of all wars.' It was an inspired hope, and the pope's sad death at Ancona, where the crusading forces which he had spent so much effort to muster were already beginning to melt away, took place at the very moment when he was making the most grandiose gesture of his life. But it was in reality more of an end than a beginning, though the pope could never admit it. Harping as always on this, his great obsession,

114

90 Pius II arriving in 1464 at Ancona, where the preparations for the crusade ▶ depended upon the arrival of the Venetian fleet. In the summer months of waiting the plague reduced the already diminished forces. The ships eventually arrived – too late – on 12 August, two days before the pope's death

he spoke for a generation which was passing, just as Nicholas of Cusa, who died the same year, spoke for one which was coming. Pius, said Cosimo de' Medici rather unkindly, was 'an old man engaging in a young man's enterprise.' But the enterprise also belonged to older men. The pope's dream of an ecumenical crusade against the Turk was alien to a new generation which was becoming increasingly ready to live alongside the aggressor, to co-exist with the world of Mohammed: a generation which, if it was hardly likely as a whole to sympathize with pacifist ideas, was less and less ready to join in a general war to extend or even defend the bounds of Christendom. Discussion, conference, concord: these were more meaningful than the idea of the crusade. Pius spoke and acted as the last representative of a different age, and one which was nearly over. The foundations of this hoped-for war had been laid in other centuries – it could not be fought in his own.

The experience of books and travel alike brought new classes of people in this age new confidence, as well as new doubts. It was a period in which there was more reading and more travelling than at any earlier period of the Middle Ages. The result was an increase of informed opinion, talk and discussion, and greater questioning over a wide range of topics, and the exchanges stimulated by travel helped to modify the opinions of many different individuals. Despite the continuance of intolerance, persecution and extremism, belief was growing in the agreement attainable through argument, in the power of books, and in peaceable persuasion. Nicholas of Cusa and Reginald Pecock were alike convinced that those whom others looked upon as adversaries should rather be treated as open-minded disputants. Words as well as wars: there were plenty of both in medieval times but they were beginning to be related in ways which show the advance of Europe upon Christendom. It took the Reformation to prove that the force of polemic could itself make war and shape international politics, but the passion and the processes were at hand long before – and so were some of the questions.

IV THE LAYMAN'S VOICE

The layman is made of clay, but even more so is the cleric who causes evil deeds to be done in imitation of himself.

JOHN GOWER (*c.* 1380)

Princes, ecclesiastical and secular alike, and counts and knights should only possess as much as common folk, then everyone would have enough.

HANS BÖHM (1476)

The uncertainties of life in the fifteenth century were public as well as private. It was a period of challenge to governmental forms. Church and state alike suffered from conspicuous disorders and in both cases unsettlement led to searching appraisals of established traditions and to experimentation with new ways. Monarchies appeared more assailable, popular insurrections more probable. In 1410 there were three contestants for the German imperial title; from 1378 to 1409 there were two rival popes and from 1409 to 1417 there were three; in the later 1430s the conciliar movement, which was generated by efforts to end the papal schism, itself became divided. Royal families in this age, compared with the thirteenth century, were more easily made and unmade. In England the century which began with the deposition and death of the last Plantagenet brought three further changes – or exchanges – of dynasty, and in the struggles of the latter part of the century two kings and two heirs to the throne lost their lives. In Bohemia, where religious upheaval added to secular dislocation, there were long periods when the country was kingless, and the estates gained in authority by electing six kings in the course of a generation. In the kingdom of Naples there were no fewer than five changes on the throne in the two years 1494–6.

There had been anti-popes, rival emperors and contested thrones before this in the history of the west, but the challenge to authority in the later Middle Ages went deeper. The sound of contest was louder and the status of the participants was changing. Personal struggles were accompanied by constitutional experiments of a kind which left an indelible impression long after they were over. And disillusion caused by the degeneration of public affairs was felt throughout society, for it was not only intellectuals and statesmen who gave expression in this period to ideas of sweeping reform. Those who talked and acted in the hope of redressing governmental wrongs included some of the humble as well as the great. The ideas of laymen – even the lowly – were acquiring greater influence; and by the end of the century, when new, stronger régimes were taking the place of the old, the shift in the balance of society was beginning to receive recognition. New voices were holding their own.

Nowhere, probably, was the prevalent attitude of questioning towards constituted authority more obvious than in the church. The fifteenth century began with one form of ecclesiastical schism and ended with another. In 1400 the church was divided in leadership; in 1500 it was divided in worship. Between the efforts of contemporaries to put an end to the forty-year-old schism in the papacy, and the crusades and negotiations directed towards bringing the Hussites back into the Catholic fold, there were many other divisions. The most notable dilemma of the century, and the one which left the largest scar on the church's consciousness, was the movement which we know as the conciliar movement: the confrontation of papacy and council which at its simplest can be seen as a struggle for different constitutional forms in the church, but which itself reflected the wider problems and divergences it was trying to settle.

A common background lay behind the most challenging movements of the later Middle Ages, secular and ecclesiastical. In insurrection and monarchical revolution, in the growth of heretical movements and the developments in the church councils, it is possible to discern parallel struggles of lay opinion to make itself heard. Among the most important questions was the right of all kinds of laymen to be listened to, as well as to speak, upon high affairs. In general the answers were conventional and in the latter part of the century papal authority was re-established, and more powerful monarchies emerged in France, Spain and England. Yet there had to be both repression and recognition. The voices of those who, when they spoke, uttered sedition or radical innovation were silenced or dismissed. While the Hussite movement became heresy, some of the most positive spiritual forces of the day became increasingly introverted. What conciliarism did not manage to conciliate was to be more explosively formulated in the changed church of a later period. Reformation succeeded where reform had failed.

'John Hus,' the king of the Romans admonished the Bohemian leader at the Council of Constance, 'no man lives without sin.' It was an injunction which could well have been addressed to other contemporaries. Those who were never called upon to die for their opinions, as Hus did at Constance on 6 July 1415, agreed with many of the premises of the heretics who did. The challenge of individual judgment to the constituted order of the church, obedience to the court of individual conscience in preference to the court of Rome, were attitudes which extended far beyond the stand taken by Hus and Jerome of Prague in 1415–16, and far beyond the heretical movements of the century. 'There is no reverence, no obedience', as Pius II expressed it at a moment of particular despondency. 'Pope and emperor are considered as empty titles and ornate figureheads.' From highest to lowest, in church and in state, office-holders in this period were subjected to a rising tide of criticism and abuse. If our only standards of judgment were the judgments of contemporaries it might indeed seem that the later Middle Ages was a period of absolute decline.

The talk of a period, like the talk of an individual, is a guide to predominant ways of thinking. Conversation helps to shape events as well as being shaped by them, and all societies gossip – though not all can be listened to equally easily. By the fifteenth century the opportunities for listening in to contemporaries have increased, and there can be no doubt that the clergy, from pope to parish priest, came high on the list of gossip-worthy subjects. No holds were barred to the inquisitive, critical layman, and those who knew the worst were seldom restrained in expressing it. Relatively few enjoyed the opportunities of Poggio Braccolini, whose scurrilous *Facetiae* reported the sort of scandalous tales which were told inside the papal

91 Aeneas Silvius Piccolomini – Pius II – did not enter the priesthood until he was over forty. His life had been that of a cultured man of the world, and the most famous of his writings became his *Eurialis et Lucretia* (The Tale of Two Lovers) a love story which reflected topically on his own past. Its popularity increased after he became pope (although he apologized for it) and this German edition of 1477 is one of many translations

court, but nobody lacked the chance to poke fun at a priest of some sort. 'One can never speak ill enough of the Roman curia,' wrote Francesco Guicciardini, who combined disillusion and belief in a way which was characteristic of his generation. Never before, probably, had reforming zeal and violent recrimination been so intimately associated. It was St Bridget of Sweden who denounced the pope as a murderer of souls, 'like to Lucifer in envy, more unjust than Pilate, harsher than Judas, and more abominable than the Jews,' and Savonarola, lecturing to an audience in Florence, who said that 'the tonsure is the seat of all iniquity. It begins in Rome, where the clergy make mock of Christ and the saints.' In this period, age-old pulpit violence, for all the conventional tone of such castigations, gained new weight through the evident disturbance in the church. The range of talkers and doubters was widened.

> I have yherde hiegh men . etyng atte table,
> Carpen as thei clerkes were . of Cryste and of his mightes,
> And leyden fautes uppon the fader . that fourmed us alle,
> And carpen ageine clerkes . crabbed wordes.

Such ecclesiastical converse did not only take place on the high tables where William Langland observed it. The taste for theological discussion reached far down into the lower reaches of society where

120

weavers and woolmen, ploughmen and labourers were arguing in fields and taverns about the nature of the soul, the sacraments, and the definition of the church. There was nothing inherently unhealthy about such gossip and no medieval century can have been without it. Yet, occurring at different levels among different sorts of people, it was associated in this period with social change and with shifts of belief.

Laymen talked. They talked – as no doubt they always had done – about church and clergy. But if their talk in the fifteenth century was in some ways more dangerous, as well as more noticeable and more interesting, this was at least in part because it was becoming better informed. The clergy were still obviously to a very large extent the purveyors of lay knowledge, but laymen themselves were (as we have seen) increasingly finding their way directly to the sources of belief. And even clerical sermons, falling on the ears of the critical or well-informed, might stimulate more doubts than they allayed.

92 This woodcut of Savonarola preaching to a congregation in Florence Cathedral, from his *Compendio di revelatione* (1495), illustrates his own description of the rapt attention of his audiences, and also the separation of men and women by a curtain at sermons

Much preaching of the time, remarked Vespasiano de Bisticci, 'stirs up doubts and does not stick to absolute statements without suggesting questioning in the form of disputation.' More important, however, than sermons was the increasing penetration into all classes of society of the consciousness and use of books. Knowledge is among the forms of possession which enlarge a sense of security and, as people in the fifteenth century were vividly beginning to realize, can itself be an agent of dangerous social change. The opportunities for secular education were growing enormously not only in the shape of more universities and books, but also in schools and public libraries, such as the town libraries of Leipzig, Hamburg and Frankfurt. Those who could read, or had access to the world of books, felt more capable of talking to their ecclesiastical superiors as equals, or even from a vantage-point of superiority. Heretics of the humblest social standing, armed with the Bible, felt equipped to challenge a bishop on the basis of divine justice. And the subversiveness of lay literacy was demonstrated by some of these radicals, who tried to implement plans for ecclesiastical renovation by broadcasting literature calling for revolution.

The purveying of knowledge had never been solely the preserve of the clergy but it was markedly less so in this age. In some ways the advance of education was associated with a movement away from the church. When in 1501 Jacob Wimpfeling took up the idea of the famous Strasbourg preacher, Geiler of Kaisersberg, and proposed the foundation of a 'gymnasium' in the city, he answered the objection that the school might lead to an increase in the number of priests.

94 Duke Federigo and his son Guidobaldo, with others in attendance, listen to a lecture at Urbino. The lecturer is probably Paul of Middelburg, a Dutch theologian and astronomer

There need be no fear, he said, for the courses were intended for those who would follow civil professions. While the openings for those with Castiglione's courtly ambitions were expanding north as well as south of the Alps, provision was also being made for the literary aspirations of humbler classes. In the early fourteenth century Giovanni Villani noted the large numbers of children in Florence who (apart from those receiving a traditional Latin education) were learning to read and write in the vernacular. In England in 1483, when Archbishop Rotherham of York made arrangements for the teaching of writing and accounting as well as of grammar in the chantry college which he founded in his native town, he made express mention of the Yorkshire youths he had in mind whose intelligence was worthy of schooling, even though they 'do not all wish to attain the dignity and elevation of the priesthood.' In a more famous school with a more famous founder the first head was chosen out of preference from the ranks of married laymen. John Colet appointed

123

◀ 93 Humanist educators aimed to make learning more enjoyable. In this school-room, painted by Holbein, the master still holds a birch but there is a sense of co-operative enterprise and on the other side of the room a girl is learning from the master's wife

95, 96 John Colet, shown in this miniature kneeling before St Matthew, first met Erasmus (seen above in Holbein's roundel) at Oxford in 1499. When Erasmus left England after another visit in 1506, he entrusted Colet's scribe with his new Latin translation of the New Testament

William Lily the high master of St Paul's in 1512, being convinced (according to Erasmus) that among such married persons was to be found 'the least corruption.' By no means all the educational advances of the time were made at the expense of the clergy, but there was a connection in some cases between doubts about clerical virtues and the growth of secular opportunities.

Public opinion helped to revalue as well as to devalue ecclesiastical office. The conviction that office depended upon merit, and that merit could be judged, gained ground in many circles, heretical and otherwise. The expansion of the lay world at the expense of the ecclesiastical altered ways of thinking about and applying the differences of standard for clergy and laity. 'The vicar of Christ', asserted a memorandum circulated at the Council of Constance in which Pope John XXIII was deposed for a whole catena of crimes, ranging from heresy and simony to murder, sodomy and fornication,

124

97 The first Pope John XXIII was imprisoned for several years after his deposition by the ▶ Council of Constance in 1415. He died in 1419 in Florence where Cosimo de' Medici later erected this bronze monument to him in the baptistery

'the vicar of Christ is bound even more than an inferior to follow Christ.' It was not only popes, however, who were judged and condemned. All orders of the church were privileged and bound by obligations of virtue higher than those of laymen. As Pius II remarked to a Florentine ambassador, 'the people expect the clergy to be so much more righteous than the laity.' Traditionally they had been taught to do so, but it was a sign of failing respect for established tradition that many ordinary laymen, scrutinizing their priests with a challenging worldly appraisal, were not prepared to allow for orthodox distinctions between the effectiveness of office and personal merit. If a priest was no better than a layman then (so current opinion tended to run) he was worse, since his calling imposed higher demands. The foundation of the Unity of the Czech Brethren, who separated from the Utraquists in Bohemia in 1467, stemmed above all from fears of the dangers of evil priests and the belief that sacerdotal office depended upon virtue. One did not have to be unorthodox to think that even if the Mass was unaffected by the ministrant's sins, prayers for the dead might be prejudiced. 'But the preyere hath no myght/For hys lyfe ys nat clene dyght,' said a work of religious instruction. Various testators, in providing for prayers to be said for their souls, made specifications about the moral qualities of the priests who were to say them. It is indicative of the mistrust of this age – as well as of its piety – that when, at the beginning of the fifteenth century, Francesco Datini (1335–1410) left a large fortune to establish a foundation for the poor of Prato, he particularly stipulated (egged on by his friend Lapo Mazzei) that no control of any sort should be excercised over it by the authority of the church or by any members of the clergy.

The behaviour of the modern church was contrasted (as reformers always contrasted it) with that of the early church whose standards were purer, in which poverty not pomp was the rule, and where everything, as it seemed, was so much better. 'In the primitive church the chalices were of wood, the prelates of gold; in these days the church has chalices of gold and prelates of wood,' declared Savonarola in a sermon, repeating an old remark. It was, in fact, an ancient concept with an infinite capacity for inspiring new actions. The possibility of regenerating the church by returning to earlier simplicity stimulated a number of reforming idealists in this period – as it had in earlier periods – from Savonarola himself to the Brothers of the Common Life, from Wycliffe to the Hussites. This kind of historicism also provoked varying degrees of alienation from the church. On the one hand it reinforced innocent suggestions like that of Gerard Zerbolt (1367–98), an influential leader of the Brothers of the Common Life at Deventer, who advocated the practice of non-sacramental confession of venial sins among laymen. On the other hand there were the more fundamental movements for reform which, following the lead of Wycliffe and Hus, became heretical.

Heresy in all periods is a reflection of orthodoxy. It was differences of degree rather than differences of kind which caused the separation of Wycliffe and Hus from the church. They were condemned most particularly for the challenging content and implications of their views upon the church. But their search for redefinition was shared by many contemporaries who were likewise turning away from office and hierarchy towards the more spiritual concept of a universal congregation, in which the distinction between priest and lay was less important than the distinction between saved and damned.

Wycliffe and Hus differed in many things apart from their personalities, circumstances and fates. Wycliffe, despite the contemporary condemnation of his views, had secured immunity for his person during his lifetime by silence, and died in peaceful possession of his Leicestershire rectory of Lutterworth. It was not until many years after his death, by which time the Bohemian movement – which had made its own use of his ideas and writings – had added to his fame as a heresiarch, that his bones were exhumed and burnt as ordered by the Council of Constance. Yet Wycliffe and Hus – and their successors – shared common aspirations. They were united above all in the concern to redefine the nature of the church. The essence of the case against Hus at Constance was derived from his work *De Ecclesia*, in which he had adapted and developed Wycliffe's writing on this question, as well as adopting the Englishman's definition. 'The holy catholic, that is, universal church is the body of all the predestined, past, present and future.' The emphasis was upon the invisible more than the visible church.

Wycliffe's ideas, repetitious, ambiguous and ambivalent here as elsewhere, can be variously interpreted from what he says about the church and the priesthood. Yet there can be no doubt that in carrying his Augustinianism to extremes in emphasis upon the church as the spiritual communion of the faithful predestined, Wycliffe not only depreciated the authority of pope and hierarchy, but also exalted the role of the pious layman. The invisible congregation of the redeemed bore no necessary relation to the visible hierarchy of the established church. The statement itself was unimpeachable,

98 Fifteenth-century chalices were often very elaborate. This Spanish example bears the arms of Gonzalo Davila, a servant of Ferdinand and Isabella

99 The Týn Church in the market square of the old town at Prague was the chief church of the Hussites. Until 1623, when it was removed by the Jesuits, there was a statue of George of Poděbrady pointing upwards with a sword to a chalice

but the deductions which could be drawn from it might be other-wise. Although Wycliffe seems at times to have accepted the orthodox view that benefits could be derived even from the ministra-tions of sinful priests, elsewhere his teaching allowed for the layman's acting as priest. The saved layman was capable of hearing confes-sions, giving pardon, even being pope: 'It is evident, logically, that a layman can be pope.' He advanced to the point of questioning the need for the hierarchy to exist at all. 'The ship of Peter is the church militant . . . nor do I see why the said ship of Peter might not in time consist purely of laymen.' Every Christian had his obligation to Christ and that obligation was definable primarily through the pre-cept of scripture, which came above and before ecclesiastical office and sacrament. The Bible more than the pope was the rock of the faith. It was the heritage of everyone, and everyone ought to know it.

Hus made his own use of the writings of the English master. Although in general more moderate, in some ways he made the challenge to authority more explicit. John Gerson (1363–1429), chancellor of the university of Paris, thought he found in Hus's *De Ecclesia* (which was written in 1413) the 'most pernicious error' that 'no sinner living in a state of mortal sin has lordship or jurisdiction or power over any of the Christian people.' He may have been doing an injustice to the actual words of the work, but its general content justified his alarm. For Hus, although admitting that the members of the church can be known only imperfectly and confusedly, and though asserting that it was the very greatest presumption for any-one to call himself a member of the church, did give believers their own criteria for judging the church militant. Many matters had, Hus agreed, to be taken on trust, but there was one infallible canon of faith which was open to all – scripture. 'Every Christian is bound to believe explicitly and implicitly all the truth which the holy spirit has placed in scripture,' and likewise he was not bound to believe any papal bulls or other writings unless they were founded upon scripture. It was not necessary to salvation, according to Hus, to believe the pope to be head of the church, since his title was nowhere expressed in scripture, and every pope who lived contrary to Christ earned the name of Antichrist as much as any layman. The pope who was avaricious could not be the true servant of Peter any more than cardinals who amassed benefices, consumed the goods of the poor, and failed to preach, could be true successors of the Apostles. And true believers in the end could not be passive believers. They had an obligation to act because criteria for active criticism were available. Revelation was indeed needed to distinguish fully between the true pastor and the false pastor, but his works could be compared with the law of Christ and 'if he seems to live contrary to Christ, how can it be judged otherwise than that he is the vicar of Antichrist?' There was, in fact, some possibility of distinguishing the true church from the false church. It was an individual forum of judgment which spelt heresy to the church.

> Therefore [wrote Hus] every faithful disciple of Christ ought to consider when the pope issues an order whether this is expressly the order of any apostle or the law of Christ, or has any foundation in the law of Christ, and recognizing this to be the case he ought reverently and humbly to obey such an order. But if he truly recognizes that the order of the pope goes counter to the order and counsel of Christ, or turns to any harm of the church, then he ought boldly to resist, lest he should become a partner in crime by reason of consent.

100 Hus, having been divested and degraded from each order of the priesthood, is led to his death (below) wearing the heretic's paper crown with the word *heresiarchia*

101 The use of mobile wagon fortresses as adapted by the Taborite warrior John Žižka (d. 1424) had an important influence on the tactics and discipline of the Hussite armies

The subject's obedience to his ecclesiastical superior was limited, in fact, by his own interpretation of the scriptural text. He was not bound to obey a prelate whom he judged to be transgressing this ultimate standard; Christ's pattern provided him with the pattern of disobedience. Moreover this was more than a theory of passive resistance, of refusal to perform the unjust orders of an unjust superior. It also entailed the active duty to correct such an errant superior. 'It is evident,' Hus went on, 'that the subject may with prudence by the rule of charity correct an erring superior and bring him back to the way of truth.'

The theories of the heresiarchs, when transmitted to their admirers and followers, received differing degrees of implementation in the course of the fifteenth century. In Bohemia Hus's ideas were grafted on to, as well as derived from, an indigenous reforming movement which fragmented after his death into divergent branches. The radical wing which produced the social experiment of Tabor proved to be less effective in the end than the moderate element, which was united particularly in the demand (sanctioned but not originated by Hus, and recognized in 1433 by the Council of Basel) for communion in both kinds: that the laity should receive the chalice with the sacramental wine as well as the bread at the eucharist – hence the name of Calixtines or Utraquists by which they were known. In England heresy also became deeply rooted but its programme was less clear and its hold much weaker. The differences between the English and Bohemian movements became more conspicuous than their earlier similarities. While the public aspirations of the English Lollards faded away ingloriously as the century wore on (and they earned the stigma of social revolutionaries with little to show for it), the Hussites ended with the fame of proscription as the first national movement for reform to sever its Roman obedience with the help of monarchic support. In both countries heresy meant revolution, but whereas in England it ran counter to and was suppressed by secular authority, in Bohemia it became itself an agent of governmental change. But though the religious struggles of the two regions had such different outcomes they were based upon some of the same premises. In both cases – though far more notably in Bohemia –

ecclesiastical office was challenged by lay intervention. In both cases the desire to regenerate the church was intimately associated with violent efforts to reduce its temporal possessions, lands and goods. Disendowment was (as it usually is) an integral part of reform.

That the Hussites succeeded where the Lollards failed was due more to political differences between Bohemia and England than to different heretical aims. Those who (however misguidedly) regarded themselves as true followers of Wycliffe – artisans and humble tradespeople for the most part, with whom the Oxford theologian would have found little in common – were as anxious as the reformers who followed Hus to redeem the church by eradicating the errors which stemmed from its earthly possessions. This matter formed one of the Four Articles of Prague which, after being formulated in 1420 and acknowledged by all parties of the Hussites, became, in the modified shape of the 'Compacts' agreed on at Basel, the rallying point of Bohemian reform for the rest of the century. The third of the articles stipulated that priests should be deprived of illegal temporal possessions and should live according to the precepts of scripture, after the example of Christ and the Apostles. In the tumultuous years 1419–25, when the Hussites managed to establish control over the political as well as the religious scene in Bohemia, this article was realized to the extent that a large proportion of the property of monks and clergy was forcibly removed from them, and passed into lay ownership. This aspect of the Hussite revolution – although it did not remain unaltered, since from the 1430s numbers of monastic and secular clergy returned to their positions – was for long one of the problematical points of difference between the Bohemians and Rome. In England the failure to accomplish anything on this same central issue accounts for the aspirations and the desperation of Lollard radicals. It led one wing of the movement from moderation to extremism. Abortive attempts to achieve by revolution what could not be reached in other ways culminated in the efforts of deluded artisans to topple Lancastrian kings from their thrones. Some of the humble Lollard plotters against Henry V and Henry VI in 1414 and 1431 were accused of having plans not only for the suppression of kings, lords and religious orders, but for the governmental and territorial positions to which they themselves were to succeed. Whereas the Bohemian nobility was able to gain through heresy at the expense of crown and church, England's king and lords stood together against what came to seem a common threat.

Lollards and Hussites differed most notably in the extent to which they came to realize a church. The exaltation of the Bible could take many shapes and inspire many sorts of separatism. Freedom to preach the word of God was a major emphasis in both movements, but the demand led in Bohemia to far greater participation by laymen in the affairs of the church and produced, in fact, one of the major problems of the Hussites – the question of their apostolic succession. In October 1435 a committee of reformers elected John Rokycana as archbishop of Prague, thereby breaking with ecclesiastical tradition – as the Taborites had already done in revolutionary style in 1420. English heretics could never begin to envisage such a triumphantly challenging action. The furthest they went – and that extremely rarely – was to resort to illicit ceremonies of ordination. The church of the Lollards, so far as it existed at all, consisted in more purely spiritual qualities – the Biblical studies of groups of laymen seeking the word of God. It did not challenge office by office so much as by belief. 'The church is not in men by way of power or dignity spiritual or temporal,' wrote one of the Lollards, 'for many princes and high bishops and others of lower degree, state or dignity are found to be apostates . . . wherefore the church consists of those persons in whom is knowing, and true confession of faith and truth.'

The confusion which results from the search for new standards of judgment resulted in paradoxical as well as tragic situations in the fifteenth century. Hus's death reflects one such paradox, the ultimate rejection of the Hussites another. The Council of Constance which condemned Hus also condemned what Hus condemned. It was striving for ends which he was striving for, and itself gave expression to some of the views which it castigated in burning him. In both cases reform in head and members ended in decapitation of the head. The council deposed Pope John XXIII; Hus was burnt for his challenge to ecclesiastical authority, particularly to the headship of the pope. Half a century later the confrontation recurred, with an

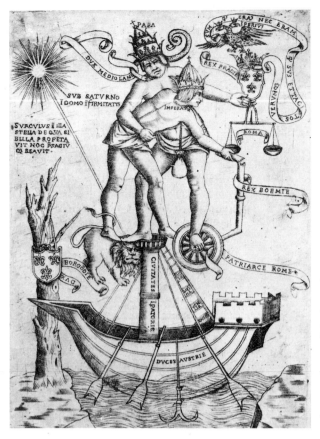

102 An allegorical engraving of *c.* 1470 alludes to the meeting in Rome in 1468–9 of Paul II and Frederick III: the mast of imperial cities (the power the papacy had gained in Germany); the ship (the dukes of Austria who had been emperors for two generations); the pair of scales (Rome); the wheel (Patriarch of Rome); the broken spindle (king of Bohemia). The engraving refers to the excommunication of George of Poděbrady by Paul II in 1466, after which Frederick hoped to gain papal recognition of his claims to Bohemia and Hungary; but the pope supported Matthias Corvinus, king of Hungary, as claimant to Bohemia

ironical twist. In 1465 Paul II confirmed and carried through the measures to deal with Bohemia which his predecessor, Pius II, had initiated shortly before his death. George of Poděbrady, whose election to the throne in 1458 had rested implicitly upon his support among Utraquist reformers, was excommunicated, declared a notorious heretic, and his subjects were freed from their oaths of obedience. Two years later the proscribed 'son of perdition', whose errors were equated with those of Waldensians, Wycliffites and other notorious sects, appealed against this sentence to a successor of the very body which had been responsible for the death of Hus and the burning of Wycliffe's bones – to a general council to be called according to the provision for such meetings made by the Council of Constance.

The conciliar movement as a whole was an attempt to redefine as well as to reform the church. From its inception it embodied the general desire of society as a whole, lay and clerical alike, not only to establish unity in the church by ending the papal schism, but also to modify absolute papal monarchy. In the end the aim of unity was reached at the expense of constitutional change. In 1449, when the Council of Basel dissolved itself and the last anti-pope in papal history resigned, the period of councils, of schism, and of attempted reform was over. The successors of Eugenius IV (1431–47) were able to restore papal authority, remake papal splendour at Rome and banish the unpleasant spectacle of conciliarism to the arena of threats and arguments. Yet in solving one set of problems the conciliar movement had succeeded in generating another, which took longer to settle. The councils represented a double challenge to the traditional order of the church. They confronted papal absolutism with representative elements, and they increased the opportunities for lay persons to deal with the affairs of the church. From the meeting of the Council of Constance (1414–18) – which was called ostensibly by John XXIII (who was to find it, in his own reported words, a trap to catch foxes) but in fact at the instance of the king of the Romans – down to the election at the Council of Basel (1431–49) of the retired duke of Savoy to take orders as the anti-pope Felix V, the councils experienced a steady increase of lay influence. The very size and publicity of the conciliar meetings – as well as the notoriety of some of the scandals they were called upon to settle – ensured widespread lay interest in their affairs. As time went on lay leaders also played a more active part in the proceedings. The councils were subjected to invasion by the same secular pressures as those which, in other ways and circumstances, transformed academic originality into popular heresy. They were at the mercy of some of the very forces which were condemned in the person of Hus.

Conciliarism was an expression of the church as the community of all the faithful. That the church (the *ecclesia*) in its widest and most general sense could be taken to be the corporate union of all Christian believers was a long-accepted theory. In practice, however, ecclesiastical government rested with the pope and the hierarchy. Such place as was allowed for a council in this hierocratic formula was for an oligarchic council of cardinals, representative only in the sense that the cardinals could themselves be regarded as representative of the whole Christian community. It was a council of this sort which met at Pisa in 1409, summoned by the united cardinals of the two rival popes on the grounds that neither pope could hold a council which would be representative of the universal church. But as time went on the issues broadened. What began by being a question primarily of oligarchy *versus* monarchy became a matter of defining the church which affected the faith of all believers. The failures and divisions of the cardinals (which had been responsible for electing the first anti-pope of 1378 and which in 1409 created a third pope), together with the failings of the popes, nearly ended by giving the church a new form of government, one in which the voices of the faithful were more corporately and less hierarchically expressed. A new concept of the congregation of the faithful emerged, in which personal qualifications withstood the claims of office. The interested layman appeared alongside the ordained churchman; decisions seemed in danger of becoming a matter of counting all heads, rather than the heads that mattered. An image of a constitution emerged, in short, which had the appearance of something more representative. This was the most startling outcome of the conciliar movement in the first half of the century, and it was the realization of it which provoked and helped the papal restoration in the mid-century.

Between the summer of 1409, when the Council of Pisa vainly proclaimed the deposition of Gregory XII and Benedict XIII, and the war *à l'outrance* which developed in the 1430s between Eugenius IV and the Council of Basel, the theory of conciliar supremacy became fully explicit. It was effectively conceived and brought to birth in the university of Paris, where one of its chief proponents was John Gerson. He was chosen to preach at Constance when the whole assembly was jeopardized by the flight of John XXIII, and he justified the actions of the general council as representing the will of the whole church. 'The church or the general council which represents it is the rule handed down from Christ, according to the directions of the Holy Spirit, so that . . . even the pope is bound to hear and obey it,' and 'though it cannot destroy the plentitude of papal power, the general council can none the less place certain limits to its use, for the good of the church.' These views found official expression in two important decrees issued at Constance. *Sacrosancta* proclaimed in April 1415 that the general council, acting as and representing the whole church, 'holds power immediately from Christ, and is owed obedience in those matters which pertain to the faith by all, of whatever estate or dignity, even papal.' The decree *Frequens* of October 1417 provided for future councils by enacting that they should meet first after five, then seven, and thereafter every ten years. Provision had been made for the continuance of a new form of government in the church. As the Council of Basel clearly demonstrated when it renewed these enactments, the issue had been joined. Who could doubt, asked Nicholas of Cusa, that the whole council is superior to the pope?

The system of deliberation and voting which was adopted at Constance was derived from university practice. Members were grouped into 'nations' (related to linguistic more than governmental frontiers), and each nation was open both to the episcopate and beneficed clergy and also to doctors of theology and law. Besides the 279 archbishops, bishops, abbots and heads of religious orders, the Council of Constance included many doctors and graduates. University representatives had an influential place alongside members of the ecclesiastical hierarchy. Education was coming to be recognized as a qualification beside ecclesiastical office – as some university men thought only proper. Also, as Cardinal Fillastre pointed out, the arguments about the incorporation of the Aragonese delegation (which arrived at Constance in 1417) raised important issues about lay representatives. 'Suppose these delegates from Aragon, who are almost all laymen and represent a lay king, were allowed as great authority in the general council as all the prelates and ecclesiastics of the realms and dominions of the same king. The idea is absurd, wrong at first hearing and contrary to nature.' It was agreed, all the same, that these secular delegates should have the power of acting and voting on behalf of the ecclesiastics of

Aragon. The Portuguese delegation, which was composed entirely of laymen with the exception of one man who was only in minor orders, raised the same question. But although Constance showed the dangers of lay participants, and even the possibility of the episcopate's being outvoted by a body of academics (who might be unbeneficed or only in minor orders), the rights and privileges of the hierarchy were preserved. Bishops and abbots always had the majority and the initiative. This council, despite the innovation of its system of voting, continued to reflect the Christian community in its traditional hierarchical form.

At Basel the case was otherwise. Here the privilege of office, corporation and nation was superseded by the weight of votes. Rank gave way to numbers. The deliberations were conducted in four commissions in which the nations were equally represented, and clerks of all ranks and dignities were admitted to the vote. Although no person could participate in the deliberations before his credentials had been examined and he had been formally admitted and incorporated, from the beginning the council had manifested its wish to receive all clerks whom it considered useful or suitable, and the meetings were flooded by a crowd of persons of lower status than the cardinals, prelates and heads of religious houses whose right to attend was incontestable. These privileged persons were outnumbered by four or five university men or lesser clergy to one of themselves. The church had long taken cognizance of professionalism but the force of this was now encountered with a vengeance, and not everyone found it agreeable. Basel had reduced everything to numbers and arithmetic, said Nicholas of Cusa, who was one of the leading churchmen who changed sides, and who turned into the 'Hercules' of Pope Eugenius as the result of his experiences at the council. At Basel, moreover, even lay persons managed to gain admission to record their vote, to the shocked surprise of Piero del Monte, a twenty-nine-year-old Roman clerk, who noted that even domestics and, worse still, married laymen were able to vote in the general congregations, as well as in the deputations. Yet some contemporaries were prepared to defend the spokesmen of the faithful even in the shape in which they appeared at

137

Basel. The voice of a canon, it was argued, was as good as that of a bishop, and an ordinary graduate could do more for the reform of the church than a cardinal. Here was something which began indeed to look like representative government in the church. And a good many people, for whom any move in this direction was nothing less than subversion, reacted with predictable horror.

To some observers the developments in the Council of Basel represented the triumph of the mob and of the uninstructed layman in the affairs of the church. A cook appeared to have become the equal of a cardinal. 'Whatever this raging mob decrees is ascribed to the holy spirit,' wrote Ambrogio Traversari about the council in 1436; of more than five hundred members there were barely twenty bishops and the rest were lower clergy or laymen so that 'the voice of a cook, so to speak, has as much value as that of a bishop or archbishop.' 'God preserve the church from mob domination or indirect domination by the secular princes,' was the prayer of John Torquemada, who had witnessed with sorrow in his heart the 'shameful doings' at the Council of Basel and the right to vote of the lower orders of the hierarchy. He thought that there could be no greater danger for the faith and the peace and unity of the church. Basel seemed to have turned the ecclesiastical world topsy-turvy. The councillors of Venice, surveying the future with a diplomatic eye in September 1433, fully endorsed the Emperor Sigismund's critical viewpoint. 'Whereas other councils used to be celebrated by mitred bishops, in this council appeared not only cardinals, archbishops, bishops and abbots, but also priors, archpriests, archdeacons, priests, and other clerks, masters of theology, doctors, even servants, and all men even of the meanest condition who wished to enter.' Those contemporaries who acted on their indignation certainly did not underestimate the dangers.

Yet for all the strangeness of these secular trespassers, and for all the reversal of form and appearance after the Council of Basel, the clock could not be completely put back. The restored papal monarchy had to recognize the claims of the temporal powers, and in the series of concordats which followed those made by Martin V at Constance, different governments obtained greater rights of control

103, 104 When Martin V (left, from his tomb in Rome) was elected pope at the Council of Constance, the papacy had reached a low ebb; yet he did much to restore papal authority before he died in 1431. Leonardo Bruni, chancellor of Florence, died in 1444, when his history of the city (begun about 1415) was still not quite completed. The *signoria* had him buried according to the 'custom of the ancients', and his monument (below) represents him dressed in a toga holding his history

over such matters as taxation of the clergy and appointments to benefices. The laity in various ways in this century acquired greater influence in the affairs of the church. The forces of opinion which the papacy rejected in both conciliarism and heresy, though they might for the moment be excluded, could not ultimately be suppressed.

The church councils were not the only places which startled contemporaries into awareness of the dangers of the multitude. While the personal authority and administrative capacities of various rulers were increasing, so also was consciousness to the politically impotent. The animated populace had to await a later generation to earn the dignity of a name, but recognition of its capacities was already dawning, and in more than theoretical form. 'Let this be an enduring lesson to the ruling men of the city; never allow the masses to take the political initiative or to have weapons at their disposal. For once they have tasted a little power, they cannot be held back.' The lesson which Leonardo Bruni emphasized for the benefit of the Florentine patriciate was derived from the revolt of the *Ciompi*, the urban

105, 106 Giuliano de' Medici (1453–78) and his brother Lorenzo (1449–92)

woolworkers, who managed by violent action in 1378 briefly to secure for themselves some representation in the government of the city. A number of other examples could have been used to drive home the same moral. From the later fourteenth century social unrest expressed itself in revolt in many different places, and, though the causes were local and various, some of the underlying influences were the same. The rebellions of the fifteenth century were less notorious than those of the fourteenth (especially the Jacquerie of 1358 in France and the rising of 1381 in England) but discontent, like plague, had become endemic, especially in certain areas. The towns of the Low Countries, with their long history of social disturbance associated with fluctuations in the weaving industry, suffered from numerous outbreaks. Bruges, Ghent and Liège all experienced unrest for a number of years in the fifteenth century. In England in addition to the Lollard contribution to disorder – which produced the abortive risings of 1414 and 1431 – the differences and disappointments associated with the end of the French war played a large part in the rising of Jack Cade in 1450. The long wars in France and Bohemia provoked local insurrections (as well as eschatological ideas), and Germany, which in the first part of the century was agitated by Hussite incursions, experienced numerous peasant revolts before the great outburst of 1525.

An aspect which was common to much of this turbulence was extreme anti-clericalism. Violent hostility to the clergy – conditioned in part by a long tradition of criticism – turned militant talk to militant deeds. If the age produced few saints of the standing of Thomas Becket it was not for lack of episcopal murders. Sudden death came to many higher clergy in the fifteenth century, sometimes on a remarkably ferocious scale. The English rebels of 1381 murdered the archbishop of Canterbury; two bishops were done to death in Cade's revolt; in the Paris riots of 1418 four French bishops lost their lives. Henry IV of England in 1405 and Lorenzo de' Medici in 1478 both got away, despite papal rumblings, with the summary execution of rebellious archbishops. At Liège, where the townsmen made an unsuccessful bid to dethrone their bishop early in the fifteenth century, a later insurrection of more serious proportions enabled them to take possession of his successor (likewise a relative of the duke of Burgundy). A few years after this outburst, in which the 'enraged citizens' had cut down various of the bishop's clerical servants, the bishop was himself murdered by an opponent and his body exposed naked in the square in front of his cathedral. Clerical orders in this century were as much of a provocation as a protection.

107 This medal was cast in September 1478 to commemorate the Pazzi Conspiracy which took place on 26 April that year. Giuliano de' Medici lost his life in the rising and Lorenzo narrowly escaped with his. The conspirators hoped to seize the government of Florence, and attacked the Medici during the celebration of Mass in the cathedral

108 The sight of a hanged man (below) would have been more familiar to most people in the fifteenth century than the scene on the right

And to those with millenarian hopes or radical aspirations the higher orders of the church seemed to demand total elimination. The ostensible aim of doing away with all the prelates of the realm was a feature of both attempted Lollard risings in England, and in 1476 Hans Böhm, the drummer-shepherd of Niklashausen near Würzburg, attacked the clergy with extreme violence in his apocalyptic preaching, conjuring up for his huge audiences the vision of a future day of reckoning when both ecclesiastical and secular princes would possess no more than common people did, and when the killing of priests would be an act of merit.

The new world envisaged by rebels and visionaries was usually a more equal world than that of harsh reality. Their view of society

142

109, 110 The miniatures of January and February from the *Très Riches Heures* of the duke of Berry show two ways of life. The duke dines in his hall protected from the fire behind him by a screen; the peasants draw as close as possible to the fire

was very different from the traditional concept of mutually inter-dependent nobility, clergy and peasantry. They saw it as dualist and divided, separated horizontally between the possessors and the possessed. On the one side lords and riches: on the other labourers and poverty.

> That one side is, that I of tell,
>   Popes, cardinals, and prelates,
> Parsons, monkes, and freres fell,
>   Priours, abbots, of great estates;
>
> . . . .
>
> The other side ben poore and pale.

143

The divisions to which the late fourteenth-century *Complaint of the Ploughman* drew attention were, as the author himself remarked, evident in 'many a country' – and mathematically as well as visually demonstrable outside England. In the 1450s, for instance, more than 80 per cent of Florentine households may be classified – from the city's tax returns – as being poor. The city of Basel was probably not unusual in that more than half of its wealth was owned by 3 to 5 per cent of the population. The voices of those who bewailed or vituperated over this state of affairs in the later Middle Ages are muffled, since they reach us largely through the mediation of others who did not share their views. But the ideas of the deprived members of society were beginning to receive fuller expression, in some cases actually to find some sympathetic understanding. Even the chronicler Froissart, who like most influential members of his generation was horrified by the doings of the English rebels in 1381, was able to put into the mouth of the insurrectionary leader John Ball a speech which sounds tolerably plausible.

> Good people, things cannot go well in England, nor will they, until all goods shall be in common and when there shall be neither villeins nor gentles, but we shall all be one. Why should he, whom we call lord, be a greater master than us? . . . They have ease and beautiful manors, and we have hardship and work, and the rain and wind in the fields; and it is through us and our labour that they have the wherewithal to maintain their estate.

By the later fourteenth century contemporaries of John Ball were beginning to express their discontent in literature as well as in rebellion. The image of the divided society, seen from beneath, reaches us through their writings and orally transmitted legends as well as through their reported deeds, and as the deprived became more articulate so the privileged became more aware of them. In addition to ballads like those of Robin Hood, which glorify the social outcast who tries to redress the balance of society by sharing among the poor the superfluous wealth of the rich, there was a literature of social injustice which grew as literacy extended. *Piers Plowman* expressed in allegorical form the crying need for regeneration, viewing from below the sufferings and wrongs in the church and the world. A more practical work of reform, which received its final shape at the time of the Council of Basel and was printed several times before the end of the century, was the *Reformation of the Emperor Sigismund*. This also propounded the case of the poor – especially the urban poor – sometimes in a radical manner. The writings of the humble Czech layman, Peter Chelčicky, are particularly significant as a sign of the times. He inherited the Bohemian tradition of social protest, but his own contribution was original, and he explicitly objected to the accepted idea of the three estates as a contradiction of Christian principles, seeing the exploitation of the working people by the nobility and clergy as opposed to the spirit of Christian charity. Like Langland, Chelčicky must have shared as well as witnessed suffering. 'Nowhere may one find rest and peace. The labouring people is stripped of everything, downtrodden, oppressed, beaten, robbed, so that many are driven by want and hunger to leave their land.'

The sufferings of the fifteenth century may have been no greater than those of earlier generations, but awareness of them is more discernible. The rich could perhaps less afford to be oblivious when the poor were expressing themselves more conspicuously, in literature as well as in revolt. Although it was not a new phenomenon for the great to describe, or be interested in, the occupations of those who worked for their leisure, some artistic productions of this age applied to social differences the increasing habit of exact observation, which was itself capable of contributing to wider social awareness. In the illuminations of the *Très Riches Heures* of the duke of Berry the differences between the seasons and the occupations appropriate to them are heightened by the contrast between the courtly activities of the protected nobles and the exposed labours of the toiling peasants. The contrast had always been there and now, as earlier, could be viewed and depicted with detachment – or even artistic enjoyment. But the sense of dichotomy was growing, particularly when experienced from beneath with passionate concern.

The weight of lay opinion was coming to count for more in many spheres. And the power of numbers was not always decried. In Florentine circles, where matters of art concerned civic pride as well as aesthetic discrimination, artists were prepared to submit themselves to the judgment of the many. The idea that there was an element of native wisdom in the untrained eye or mind of the multitude was not invented in this century, but it was allowed new scope. Machiavelli argued – and this was one of the points on which Guicciardini took issue with him – that popular opinion should have a say in matters of political choice, such as appointments to office. Relying mainly on gossip the general public was, he admitted, liable to err, but even so its judgment was safer than that of princes. 'The populace always makes fewer mistakes than do princes.' This concept of the value of a consensus to judge of professional matters was also advocated in questions of art, for instance by Alberti in his *On Painting*, or by Dürer who advised painters to listen to all criticism, including that of dull men for 'as a rule they pick out the most faulty points, while they entirely pass over the good.' To suppose that a multiple opinion would register imperfection was, in a sense, the counterpart of the idea (advocated and practised in the Renaissance) that perfection was to be found by combining into a whole the perfect units extracted from a number of parts. In practice, of course, it was to be a long time before common opinion was accorded a significant role in any of these spheres, but there were at least restricted ways in which the transformation of art and aesthetics accomplished in the Renaissance enlarged the place of lay judgment. Art and society acted upon each other at many levels and the fifteenth century notably altered their relationship.

It was an experienced and sagacious fifteenth-century pope who wrote that 'nothing is more perilous than to examine the actions of popes.' In this century such examinations had been conducted with the utmost publicity and the result as well as the cause was the increasing audacity of secular judgment. The lay world was growing at the expense of the ecclesiastical and in both church and state accepted authorities were challenged. It was a time which was more productive of new questions than of workable new answers. 'No man', Hus had been told, 'lives without sin.' Many popes besides Pius II – looking back on his worldly days as Aeneas – could knowledgeably echo that truism, and papal sins had become public property since the days of Hus. The papacy sinned, survived and recovered, but at a price to the church which was already becoming evident long before the hot August day of 1503 when the corpse of Alexander VI, the last and most infamous pope of the century, was unceremoniously bundled into his too small coffin. It was a price from whose payment the church still suffers – the price of ecclesiastical unity.

The fifteenth century was full of alarms. Contemporaries did not moderate their phraseology in describing them, and more in general was threatened and lamented and prophesied and direly expected than was actually done. Historians are obliged by the nature of their calling to consider immobility less than change, but to many contemporaries many things seemed despairingly the same. Yet events, and views of events, did move forward. Through this period of militant challenge more people were learning the dignity or destiny of self-expression. Hus's opinion that God had 'hidden the way of truth from the wise and prudent and revealed it to laymen' accorded with the widening vision of a world which was clearly changing. It was finding more room for laymen.

111–113 Three states of human society in late fifteenth-century miniatures by Jean Bourdichon; the beggar in his hovel, the artisan in his workshop, and the lord in a princely room

V THE CHURCH AND THE WORLD

*Behold how the sun and moon are darkened so that even
the city that is set on a hill is hid and covered in darkness
that it cannot be seen, in such a way that of the infinite
multitude of Christians it would not be easy to find one
who is certain where the true church of God is.*

MATTHIAS OF JANOV (d. 1394)

I pray you, what else is a city except a great monastery?

ERASMUS (1518)

'Who loves the world hates God,' wrote Coluccio Salutati. It was an
ancient maxim which had long ruled the counsels and aspirations of
the church. Purification, whether of the individual or of society, was
an aim best pursued by retreat from the contaminating affairs of the
world. The highest life was the most dedicated monastic life, and
monks were doing for the rest of society what the majority of its
members aspired to, but were unable to do for themselves. Yet
Salutati, putting together the traditional arguments rather academi-
cally, for the benefit of a friend who had lately joined the Camaldolese Order, in a treatise 'Concerning the world and religion', which
was written about 1381, was stating a case which was in fact becoming partially outdated. The religiosity of the later Middle Ages was
increasingly expressed not so much by turning away from the world
as by exploring the means of regeneration available within it. The
ascetic contemplative ideal was being drawn into secular society
rather than itself withdrawing individuals from society. The retreats
of this age were personal more than institutional. Belief in institutions
was waning while individual religiosity was growing. 'The world is
wide enough and good enough to win heaven in,' remarked the
English mystic Richard Rolle, thereby epitomizing more clearly than
Salutati the conviction of a generation that was deeply religious as
well as deeply critical, and steadily gaining experience of the ways of
reconciling religion with the world.

149

◀ 114 San Bernardino preaching in the Piazza del Campo, Siena.
The saint holds his device of the monogram of the name of Jesus
(YHS in a halo of flames), which brought charges of heresy upon him

Ancient beliefs are usually tenacious and it was a sign of the departure of the Middle Ages when the view began to gain ground that modernity and goodness are inherently associated. Yet beside the conservatives who continued to extol and adopt the monastic way of life must be placed those individuals and movements whose ways of thought linked them more with the future than with the past. Changing attitudes towards the monastic vocation reflected changes in society, and the expansion of the layman's world was most conspicuously the expansion of towns. Urban life demanded its own ethic and in various ways it was beginning to find one. Most notably and soonest it did so in Italy.

It was in Florence that civic wealth found its first defenders and its own morality. Material possessions came to be seen as the means of virtue through use as well as through abnegation; greater recognition of man's humanity brought greater recognition of human needs. Wealth could be regarded as providing larger opportunities for the good life, for happiness, education and patronage, and when Matteo Palmieri died in 1475 he was praised for having realized 'how much riches contributed to a civic life led with dignity.' The ideas of leading Florentines had changed a great deal in the hundred years since the death of Petrarch, though Petrarch himself – with his far-reaching genius – had shown them the way. In this, as in other matters, he was prescient in being divided, and in more than one work he had shown how deeply he was troubled by the problem of reconciling his classical ideal of literary activity and retirement with the Christian ideal of contemplation and renunciation. Admiration for Cicero and St Augustine created conflict within him. Petrarch's rural seclusion at Vaucluse was a kind of ascetic retirement tempered by intense literary industry, and in both aspects it represented a withdrawal from urban distractions to rural calm. 'No place is more favourable for the meditative man than a rustic solitude,' he said, and confessed that 'I nowhere feel my mind working more happily than in the woods and mountains . . . nowhere do great thoughts occur to me more readily – if indeed a great thought ever does occur to me.' But though country strolls with his dog had helped on the *Africa,* Petrarch ended his days in the more urban environment of

Venice and Padua. And in his *Secret*, written when he was about thirty-eight in a mood of middle-aged anxiety, Petrarch chose Augustine as his interlocutor, and his self-imposed confessor took the poet to task both for his concern over material goods to provide for his old age, and for his longing to conquer mortality by literary immortality.

As time went on, and Petrarch's successors continued the work he had begun, their increased understanding of classical authors helped them to resolve this dilemma. There was no longer any need to blame Cicero (as Petrarch had blamed him) for having abandoned a life of literary exile. Life and virtue, action and contemplation, were placed in a new relationship and in a setting which was essentially civic. If 'the whole glory of virtue is in activity,' as Vittorino da Feltre remarked, quoting Cicero in a letter to Ambrogio Traversari, such activity was more 'at home in cities and towns away from solitude.' Indeed true virtue should shun selfish isolation. Vittorino da Feltre, Matteo Palmieri, Pier Paolo Vergerio, Leonardo Bruni and others called the philosopher to an active social life – in cities. Leone Battista Alberti in his treatise *On the Family* advocated bringing up children in the town rather than the country for the very reason which had led Petrarch to escape so thankfully from Avignon – so that they should become acquainted with vice as well as virtue. This age took all experience for its province.

115 Antonio Rossellino's bust of Matteo Palmieri, carved in 1468, was clearly patterned upon Roman portrait busts, as was fitting for so distinguished a Latinist. In one respect, at least, convention seems to have triumphed over accuracy for according to Vespasiano although Palmieri was favoured by a handsome presence 'he became bald when he was very young'

The philosophy of 'civility' was developed first and furthest in Italian circles and in shapes which sometimes looked more blatantly worldly than older conventions had been. But the humanists from Salutati onwards were not rejecting established religious ideals, though their concern with newer problems sometimes made them leave these on one side. Nor were these problems peculiar to Italy. To a differing degree they were also those of Europe north of the Alps. 'No human work can be better', wrote Palmieri in the 1430s in his *On Civic Life*, 'than care for the welfare of the *patria*, the maintenance of the *città*, and the preservation of unity and harmony in a rightly ordered community.' In 1498 Savonarola was burnt in Florence after the failure of his attempt to turn the city into a republic of Christ, and in the same decade that Palmieri was writing Joan of Arc was burnt at Rouen for actions in which the call of 'patria' had been delivered through the voice of the Archangel Michael. In both cases a spiritual mission took the form of an essentially public cause: Joan's was the unification of France; Savonarola's the improvement of the life and government of Florence.

The predominant forms of religious vocation change from age to age. Those of the fifteenth century, though they were often directed towards public objectives, tended to be pursued in ways which were personal and individualistic rather than through tenure of ecclesiastical office. The church still attracted its share of enthusiastic reformers – more than are often allowed for – but there were significant numbers of individuals who deliberately shrank from seeking or accepting official positions. The notorious affluence of the church and the pursuit of benefices by ambitious worldly careerists had introduced such glaring anomalies into the ecclesiastical structure, such enormous contrasts of wealth and poverty, privilege and deprivation, that many of those with a deep sense of religious vocation tended to avoid ecclesiastical promotion. One can hear a note of aggrieved resignation in the voice of Francesco Guicciardini – a man who was nothing if not ambitious – when he recorded his father's refusal to allow him in 1503, when he was twenty, to acquire any of the benefices of his late uncle (who had been archdeacon of Florence and bishop of Cortona). 'For Piero determined not to have

116, 117 Savonarola (right) reiterated prophecies of a coming scourge of God that seemed to be fulfilled in the French invasion of 1494. Many medals were cast, bearing his text and showing the sword of God brandished over a flood-threatened city

any of his sons a priest, although there were five of them, because he thought the affairs of the church were decadent.' Their awareness of the need to forge a new set of values caused some of those with the highest spiritual aspirations to fear that tenure of office might conflict with true service to individual, congregation or faith. San Bernardino of Siena (1380–1444), who came to look back on his youthful endeavours to take to the wilderness in ascetic withdrawal as a 'veritable pitfall', refused three bishoprics in the course of his career. There were contemporaries who thoroughly approved. On the first occasion the Camaldolese scholar Traversari wrote imploring him to flee this evil. Bishoprics, abbacies, offices, even cures of souls had become so entangled with worldly associations that the best spiritual currents tended to flow into other channels. Gerard Groote (1340–84) had a conception of the priesthood which was so far beyond the range of contemporary reality that he never felt able to move above the order of deacon. And he said of his follower Florence Radewijns (1350–1400), 'I was instrumental in getting only one priest ordained, and I think indeed that he was truly worthy, but I shall take good care in future not to enter on a similar step too rashly, for I see very few who are suited for this ministry.'

The idea that the church's ministry should be reformed by taking far greater care over its recruitment, that to have better priests it was necessary to have fewer, and that this was an important way of redressing the balance between church and world, had been arrived at long before the days of *Utopia*. Heretics as well as reformers, anticipating the views of More, Colet and Erasmus, had come to the conclusion that one reason why sacerdotal standards were low was simply that there were too many clergy. It would be better to have few priests, but they should be good ones, said Nicholas of Cusa, and San Bernardino expressed a similar conviction. More means worse. It was hardly an original argument but there was possibly something to it. For instance, in the diocese of Sées in Normandy the number of clerks who were ordained increased fourfold between 1445 and 1510, and there were similar increases in the dioceses of Rouen and Toulouse. Even allowing for possible growth in population it seems likely that this progression represents a change in the ratio of clergy to laity, and that it involved some lowering of standards.

'No man in these days builds churches or founds monasteries,' lamented Abbot Trithemius of Sponheim (1461–1516) with evident exaggeration in 1493. Monasteries and churches were still being founded as well as restored and rebuilt in the fifteenth century, as is demonstrable from places as different as the great monastery of the Jerónimos at Belem in Portugal or the church of St Barbara at Kutná Hora in Bohemia. There were also reforms among various branches of the Benedictine Order which joined together in the pursuit of improved observance. Such were the congregations which centred upon Valladolid and Montserrat in Spain, Melk in Austria, and Bursfeld in Germany (to which Sponheim belonged). Yet there was a sense in which Trithemius was right. Great founders might still make great monastic gestures, but the forms of endowment to which many laymen devoted their patronage in this period tended rather to be secular – chantries, hospitals, colleges and schools. Various individuals, too, can be seen rejecting the monastic vocation, convinced that to adopt it would not assist their religious aspirations.

Both Salutati and Petrarch considered the drawbacks as well as the advantages of the monastic profession, and other writers dealt

119 The convent of the Jerónimos (right), was founded in 1499 on the place where Vasco da Gama embarked for his voyage to India, to commemorate that achievement

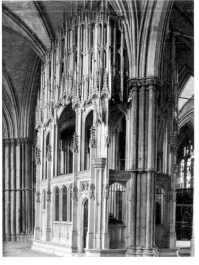

118 Bishop William Wainfleet, founder of Magdalen College, Oxford, and benefactor to Eton College of which he was provost, built his tomb and chantry chapel in Winchester Cathedral before his death in 1486

with the question with characteristic extremism. 'I simply affirm that you are no better than other men who are your equals in virtue in an active life,' wrote Lorenzo Valla in the 1430s, arguing the case against monasticism in a way which (he was careful to point out) was purely hypothetical. For others it could not be less than a matter of ardent conviction. When a friar unwisely remarked to St Catherine of Genoa (1447–1510) that his religion enabled him to love God better than she could, being wedded to life in the world, she turned on him in a passionate outburst. 'If I thought that your habit had the power of gaining me one single additional spark of love, I should without fail take it from you by force.' It was in a similar spirit that nearly two generations earlier the chancellor of Paris, John Gerson had in 1401 given advice to his six sisters. They were all resolved to dedicate their lives to religion, and it was the hope of their father that all his children would enter the church. The chancellor, however, while warmly supporting his sisters' desire for chastity and devotion, advised them to pursue their aim in devout observance round the family hearth rather than by entering a religious order. For some

155

years, until the disturbances caused by the struggles between Armagnacs and Burgundians made their existence impossible, the sisters followed Gerson's advice, living as a small lay-apostolate, reciting the offices and fasting and praying in their parental home. It was a life significant of a new generation.

Gerson, who was one of the most redoubtable reformers of his day, became involved some years after giving this advice in a public discussion upon the same issue. Together with another famous Paris chancellor and theologian, Pierre d'Ailly, he combated the arguments on behalf of a rigidly monastic dogma which were put forward at the Council of Constance by a conservative Dominican, Matthew Grabon. Grabon's thesis was that poverty, chastity and obedience could not be lawfully and meritoriously pursued outside the established religious orders. Anyone who tried to give up everything for Christ without joining such an order was endangering his soul, committing homicide and mortal sin. It was an ultra-conservative case, based upon the premise of the separation of church and world which the high medieval church had developed into tradition. For Grabon, religion* and the world stood diametrically opposed; the secular and religious lives were incompatible; it was contradictory 'for a secular to be a religious, or the other way round.' D'Ailly and Gerson, on the other hand, were the spokesmen of an entirely different viewpoint. Their conviction that the 'Christian religion is true also among seculars' was derived from a spirituality which embraced the whole of society. They made use of historical arguments to refute Grabon's narrower interpretation, pointing out that many early Christians, including church fathers, could be called 'religious' without being called monks, having lived before the days when monastic orders were founded. Monastic vows were in fact only one form of virtuous life and provided a disposition rather than a way to perfection. Indeed, argued Gerson (and it recalls the advice he had given to his sisters), though orders helped some to better observance they might actually hinder others, for whom it would have been 'safer to have remained in the world.'

* The words 'religion' and 'religious' as used in these arguments (*religio* and *religiosus*) meant 'religious orders' and those who belonged to them. The English words introduce an unfortunate but unavoidable ambiguity of meaning.

These exchanges were not simply dialectical. They were prompted by the activities of what was probably the most generative religious movement of the whole century, and one which most fruitfully expressed its defenders' modernistic outlook: the Brothers of the Common Life or (as it was also called at the time) the *Devotio Moderna*. The Brothers and Sisters of the Common Life, who developed as a group in the Low Countries round Gerard Groote and his disciple Florence Radewijns, essentially embodied the idea of a congregation which aimed to promote religious observance without separation from secular society. Groups of clerks and laymen joined together in a common devotional life, linked in their aims and activities, sharing income and expenses, but not distinguished by dress or vows, and free to depart at will. The community reflected, in fact, its founder's decision, taken in 1379, to leave the Carthusian Order (in which he had spent two years) for an active preaching ministry in Flanders, Guelders and Holland. That his step was in sympathy with his times is shown by the success of the movement which he started. 'If devout women separate themselves from the world', wrote Groote, 'and try to serve God in the privacy of their homes, without taking monastic vows, they are just as religious as nuns in their convents. To love God and worship him is religion, not the taking of special vows.' The sisterhood which Groote established in his family house at Deventer in 1374 was the beginning of a far-reaching movement which exercised a powerful influence upon lay piety north of the Alps. It centred upon works, particularly of an educational kind, to widen and enrich the religious life of laymen, as well as to prepare priests for the church.

'I dare not advise you to enter a monastery,' wrote Groote to one of his followers, 'though it is not for me to judge, being ignorant of God's ways. My desire is that you remain in the world, and be not of the world.' The desire came to be most amply fulfilled in the schools and literature of the Brothers, which carried their fame and influence far afield, from Zwolle, Deventer, Ghent and Liège to Westphalia and Saxony, to Erfurt, Paris and Rome. From the outset the movement was associated with educational work, and the manual labour to which members were specially committed was the

157

copying of texts. The 'house of Florence' at Deventer was founded by Radewijns so that – as at Zwolle – 'devout priests and clerks with a few poor laymen might live there in common from the labour of their hands, that is the work of writing.' Love of books and the ability to write were among the points on which candidates for admission were questioned, and the multiplication of religious texts for which the Brothers were responsible played a vital role in contemporary book production, and continued into the days of printing when they early established their own presses. In addition, the Brothers gained European fame for the opportunities provided for the sons of poor parents in the numerous schools which they founded or influenced. These facilities, though intended primarily for those who wished to become priests, were not limited to clerical objectives. 'We have decided to live in cities, in order that we may be able to give advice and instruction to clerks and other persons who wish to serve the Lord,' wrote the Brothers of Zwolle, who had one of the most celebrated schools, in 1415. John Cele (1350–1417), a famous teacher at Zwolle, following the belief that farmers and burghers should be able to read the Bible for themselves, invited all the inhabitants of the town to attend his courses. The modernity of the *Devotio Moderna* lay particularly in its openness to secular influences, its refusal to acknowledge dividing lines between ecclesiastical orders and the religious aspirations of laymen.

The Brothers of the Common Life were by no means hostile to monasticism. Groote himself expressed the wish that his disciples should live under an established rule, and the house founded at Windesheim in 1386, in accordance with this request, adopted the Augustinian rule. It prepared boys for the monastic life and became an influential centre for monastic reform. What the movement did, however, was to create new opportunities for, and to place new emphases on the life of laymen who sought ascetic virtues but did not wish to renounce the world. In the words of Amilius van Buren, who succeeded Radewijns from 1400 to 1404, 'although the monastic state is preferable in the opinion of the church, nevertheless he who lives a saintly life outside a monastery will receive the reward of saintliness.' It was an effort to remodel a Christian ideal which – like most reforming movements – was in part historical, trying to separate early church practices from the accretion of later tradition.

By the time Erasmus escaped in the 1480s – as it afterwards seemed, with relief – from the schools of the Brothers of the Common Life, one part at least of the movement had lost some of its earlier inspiration and become subjected to more narrow-minded views. Erasmus retained a life-long sense of resentment at the unworthy monastic pressures which had been put upon him. The times were moving forward and Erasmus came to epitomize one whole phase of their movement. Yet the schools of the Brothers at Deventer and 's Hertogenbosch in which he felt so little at home had originated in an outlook not so far removed from his own, reacting as he did against the harm done to Christian devotion by 'those orders which are called religious', and seeing it as 'more in accordance with the teaching of Christ to regard the whole Christian world as one house and, so to speak, as one monastery.' For all his later ungrateful reaction, Erasmus – like another great scholar, Nicholas of Cusa – owed a positive debt to the teaching of the *Devotio Moderna*.

Probably the most famous product of the Brothers of the Common Life was a book. The *Imitation of Christ* (perhaps more properly described as a group of treatises, though many generations have now read and valued it as a book) was conceived and compiled in the circles of the *Devotio Moderna*. Thomas Hemercken à Kempis (1379/80–1471), who probably put it together in his middle age, entered the monastery of Mount St Agnes at Zwolle when he was twenty, and spent the rest of his life there. The *Imitation* is a work which tells a great deal not only about the circles in which it was written, but also about the forms of contemporary piety more generally. As the large numbers of surviving manuscripts testify, it enjoyed widespread popularity in its own century as well as later, and many readers would have agreed with Luther, who estimated its worth beside that of the Bible and the works of St Augustine. The *Imitation* is *par excellence* the religious handbook of the fifteenth century. It is essentially a companion of the inner life, a guide for the individual Christian who wished to accompany Christ through his own mystical exercises. 'Blessed are they that enter far into inward things.' The names of the separate books are themselves revealing: from 'counsels useful for the spiritual life', it proceeds to sections 'on the inner life' and 'on inward consolation'. Three-quarters of the work is past and how much has the reader been called upon to consider the ministrations of the church? Thomas à Kempis, it is true, was an Augustinian and the *Imitation* was addressed in part to those who were living according to a religious rule. Yet the book emphasized that 'the wearing of a religious habit, and shaving of the crown do little profit' as compared with the inner transformation of the truly religious man, and it was intended for and welcomed by those whose mystical aspirations did not include renunciation of the world. The *Imitation of Christ* became popular as a 'guide to paradise' for good Christians living in the world. Its success attests the desire shared by many contemporaries to find some way of reconciling the monastic ideal with an active modern life.

Ostensibly à Kempis depreciated book-learning. 'For what are words but words? They fly through the air, but do not hurt as stone.' Divine knowledge transcends all other forms of knowledge. Yet without the assumption that reading could be a valuable aid to contemplation the *Imitation* would not have been written at all, and in presuming upon his readers' literacy the author also presumed upon their Biblical background. The book itself relied greatly upon scripture, which was the main source of its large number of quotations, and this association certainly accorded with the times. The *Devotio Moderna* gave considerable impetus to the propagation of Biblical texts and although the Bible (unlike the *Imitation*) cannot be called a best-seller in the fifteenth century, it was among the first vernacular books to be printed in German, Italian and Catalan. Before 1501 it had appeared in more than ninety Latin editions and in thirty vernacular editions in six languages. Reading was coming to play an increasingly large role in lay devotion and, for all his disclaimers, Thomas à Kempis and the movement to which he belonged helped it to do so.

The *Imitation* enjoyed its wide circulation partly by reason of the fact that, as a manual of mystical withdrawal composed in a religious context, it was so freely detachable from institutions and ceremonies.

This is also true of another book which belongs to the same family. Erasmus's *Enchiridion* was written in 1501 for an unlearned friend, in order to persuade this man of the world of the value of a life of devotion. The procedures advocated are like those of the *Imitation*. Prayer and knowledge were the foremost means of keeping Christ always in view, and knowledge meant above all 'fervent study of the holy scriptures.' Erasmus, too, has remarkably little to say – except in criticism – of ecclesiastical practices and he later thought it desirable to defend himself with the remark that 'we do not, however, anywhere condemn moderately observed ceremonies, but we cannot tolerate their being made into the prow and poop (as the saying goes) of holiness.' The fullest assurances were those that lay within. 'God is not pleased save by invisible piety.'

Devotional reading, individual meditation assisted particularly by the Bible: these formed the avenue to higher things. And after prayer and inward preparation came communion. The fourth book of the *Imitation of Christ* dealt with the sacramental centre of the faith, the eucharist. 'I shall have besides, for comfort and for the guidance of my life, the holy books, and above all these, your most holy body for my special haven and refuge.' It was the climax of the individual's colloquy with his God. Yet even here it was the individual and personal which was emphasized above all else, and the sacrament is considered in a way which sheds light on contemporary practice. Firstly it is remarkable that the act of communion is envisaged essentially as the meeting of the individual communicant with Christ. There is no idea here of the *fellowship* of communion which had once been so important – the union of all the faithful in the shared sacramental meal. Secondly there is the emphasis which the *Imitation* places upon the desirability of frequent communion, not only for priests, but for all believers. 'How happy and acceptable to God is he who so lives, and keeps his conscience so pure, as to be ready and well disposed to communicate even every day, if he were permitted.' Both emphases, though they may now not seem surprising, were highly indicative of important changes in the later medieval church – changes which reveal the growing estrangement between Christians and the ministrations of the church.

120 Carpaccio, *The Blood of the Redeemer*, 1496

121 Silver-gilt
monstrance,
French, fifteenth century

122 Sakramentshaus by
Adam Kraft in St Lorenz,
Nuremberg, 1493–6

By the beginning of the fifteenth century the eucharist had become a rare and distant rite for ordinary believers. Most of the laity communicated seldom and, when they did so, with limited understanding. And this was the official policy of the church. Frequent communion of the laity became altogether exceptional after the early centuries of the church, and doctrinal developments tended to take the sacrament further away from the congregation. Above all, the official promulgation in 1215 of the doctrine of transubstantiation, by enhancing the sanctity of both the host and the celebrant's office, added to the fear of profanation and thereby increased the separation of laymen from both altar and priest. It was provided that the laity should communicate once a year (at Easter), and although communion at Christmas and Whitsun as well was practised and advocated in some quarters in the thirteenth and fourteenth centuries, this was exceptional. Various theologians who dealt with the

123 Grünewald, detail from the Isenheim Altarpiece, c. 1513–15. Carpaccio (opposite) shows the Redeemer's blood flowing direct from the wounds into the eucharistic vessel, while Grünewald's altarpiece, painted for a hospital, graphically records Christ's physical agony

question in the high Middle Ages were against frequent communion of the laity, and persons who wished to communicate more than thrice a year had to get ecclesiastical permission. It was a rarity, so much so that frequent communicants became as much an object of official suspicion as non-communicants – the extremes of belief and disbelief could be equally dangerous. In fact total failure to communicate may have been not uncommon. The famous preacher San Giovanni Capestrano recounted in a sermon delivered in Vienna in 1451 how he had never received the sacrament (though he had often confessed) until he entered the Franciscan Order in 1415, when he was thirty. And if laymen rarely received the body of the Lord, when they did so the Latin of the Mass was in many cases beyond their comprehension. Even the privileged whose understanding had been enlarged by the help of a translation might still find themselves debarred from the central mystery of the actual consecration – those 'five words . . . that no man but a priest should read'. Respectful reverence – and reverence from a distance – this rather than understanding was the envisaged role of the layman at Mass.

Enthusiasm, however, may be increased rather than diminished by a sense of distance. Popular attitudes towards the sacrament of the altar in the later Middle Ages, though they may now be judged debased and were condemned as superstitious by contemporaries, were nevertheless the direct outcome of official ecclesiastical policy and also a sign of the vitality of contemporary piety. The doctrine of the real presence lent itself to crude interpretations. To many pious believers in the fifteenth century the reality of the presence appeared with all the actuality of drops of blood. This approach was connected with the concentration of the times upon the human aspects of the Holy Family and the physical suffering of the Passion. 'Suddenly I saw the red blood trickling down from under the garland [of thorns] hot and freshly and right plenteously . . . like to the drops of water that fall off the eaves after a great shower of rain, that fall so thick that no man may number them with bodily wit.' With these words the English mystic, Julian of Norwich, describes how she saw the crucifix held before her eyes during a critical illness in 1373. Believing was far more a matter of seeing in the fifteenth century than it has since become, and while contemporary paintings did not spare horror and bloodshed in depicting the Passion, many believers – as was evident, for example, in the numbers who flocked to see the reputed bleeding host of Wilsnack – were avid for such sights. Veneration of the five wounds of Christ was a popular late medieval devotion, with its own Mass as well as special prayers. Here too the sacrificial element of worship was emphasized with extreme physical realism. 'Drown you in the blood of Christ crucified,' St Catherine of Siena ended a letter. Blood could be the central element in spiritual vision: red the signal to inspire rapture. For St Catherine of Genoa, a saint whose life was devoted to care of the sick and destitute of her city, red was the colour of revelation, as later described by her biographer. 'Our lord, desiring to enkindle still more profoundly his love in this soul, appeared to her in spirit with his cross upon his shoulder dripping with blood, so that the whole house seemed to be all full of rivulets of that blood.' So sensitive did she become to the colour red that she had to ask a visitor who came to see her during her final illness in 1510 to go and change his scarlet robes.

Errors as well as beliefs, crudities as well as devotions, were fostered by the emphasis which the church placed upon the visual aspect of the faith. For the authorities did not only assist and inform the illiterate believer with the visual aids with which we are familiar – paintings, illuminations, sculptures, roodscreens. They also stressed the fact that seeing could have its own sacramental value. The elevation of the host immediately after the consecration which became established practice in the thirteenth century, arose from the desire to increase the visual participation of the congregation, and it was maintained in orthodox works that even 'the sight of Christ's body' brought positive spiritual and material benefits. Another aspect of visual worship, which developed spontaneously among the faithful, was reverence for the reserved sacrament – that is, the consecrated host which was kept in church for the communion of the sick or dying. In the later Middle Ages the monstrance became an important eucharistic vessel, designed for the express purpose of displaying the sacrament to the people in church, or as it was carried through the streets on such occasions. Yet the church – for all the indirect encouragement it gave to these practices – was chary of this development, and various fifteenth-century German councils, such as that held by Nicholas of Cusa at Cologne in 1452, prohibited displays and processions of this kind except at the feast of Corpus Christi. It may have been as a means of canalizing this eucharistic devotion into another, legitimate channel that the fashion arose in Germany and the Low Countries of building elaborate 'sacrament-houses', often in the form of monumental Gothic pinnacles, in which the consecrated host or the eucharistic vessel could be seen and revered in church.

While these developments show that separation from the centre of sacramental mysteries was no bar to lay enthusiasm, there was also a growing demand by the laity in the late fourteenth and fifteenth centuries for increased participation in the eucharist. A number of different individuals expressed the wish for more frequent communion. Those who shared the view of Thomas à Kempis on this matter include John Ruysbroeck, William Langland, St Catherine of Siena, Matthias of Janov, St Vincent Ferrer, Joan of Arc, St Catherine of Genoa, John Rokycana and Geiler of Kaisersberg. Savonarola, in his *Triumph of the Cross*, wrote of the marvellous and supernatural effects visible in the life, spirit and appearance of the faithful who habitually received the sacrament. Generations earlier Gerson, advocating frequent communion as the way to become practised in mystical theology, had advised his sisters to confess and celebrate as often as their devotion allowed them. Yet such a recommendation was not without its hazards. These were demonstrated to the church authorities by the developments in Bohemia where the enlarged participation of the laity in the sacrament of the altar was a central point of the reforming programme. Already in 1389 Matthias of Janov had had to renounce his view that laymen should be exhorted to daily communion, and that the drinking of the sacramental wine should be available for all, not only for priests. The Hussites' return to the Utraquism of the primitive church helped both to bind them together and to cut them off from the rest of the church. The orthodox outside Bohemia were shocked by eucharistic practices which included public celebrations in camps and fields and the administration of the sacrament to infants.

The dangers of frequent lay communion were not confined to the Hussites. Even perfectly orthodox individuals did not escape them. The conversion of St Catherine of Genoa in 1474 was closely connected, according to her biographer, with 'the desire for holy communion, a desire which never again failed her throughout the whole course of her remaining life.' From that year until her death she became a daily communicant, but it is noteworthy that this exceptionally frequent celebration did not bind her more closely to the counsels and controls of the church. Very rarely, it seems, did she confess, and she continued for many years without any regular priestly guidance. Understandably at least one person was worried about the wisdom of her behaviour, and Catherine herself, who previously had had 'at times a feeling as of envy towards priests, because they communicated on as many days as they would,' was conscious of the privilege she was claiming. The personal assurance derived through the eucharist might be combined with estrangement – even alienation – from the church. 'Did you receive the sacrament of the eucharist at feasts other than Easter?' Joan of Arc was asked. 'Pass over that,' she is reported to have replied. Some forms of enthusiasm were better not expounded to the church.

The Mass is one way of exploring the relationship of individual believers with the church. The other is the sermon. 'These two above all,' remarked Geiler of Kaisersberg, 'namely the taking of the sacrament and the hearing, reading or meditation of the divine word, are the greatest comfort and restoration of the devotion and fervour of those wearied in the way of God.' The word of God, heard and expounded as well as read, could be set beside the sacrament, and there is no doubt that listeners were numerous. It was a great age for the sermon, for preachers of every kind and degree; churches as well as pulpits were designed and built for them. The large German hall-churches provided ample space for congregations at sermons, and in Italy Leonardo da Vinci's sketches of church plans included ideas for internal theatres for preaching, in one of which the top of a column was to serve as the preacher's pulpit.

'How many benefits have come through one sermon!' exclaimed an outspoken chancellor of the university of Oxford, pointing out complacently that others, not he, had fallen short in this activity. He was certainly preaching to the converted. The call to the sermon was heard across the length and breadth of fifteenth-century Europe as clearly as any Muslim call to prayer. More people must have been delivering, hearing, writing and reading – as well as advocating – sermons in this age than ever before. It was a period in which people were both canonized and burnt for their enthusiasm for preaching. 'If I had gold enough,' said the indefatigable Margery Kempe, 'I would give every day a noble for to have every day a sermon.' It was indicative of the times that various people were prepared to go beyond the idea of the parity of Mass and sermon to assert that the Mass was less valuable than the sermon. 'For by preaching folk be stirred to contrition and to forsake sin and the fiend and to love God. . . . By the mass be they not so.' This view of the author of *Dives and Pauper* might have been echoed by many followers of Wycliffe and Hus. The view that untrammelled vernacular preaching would be a major solvent of the church's troubles, and that Anti-

124, 125 The external pulpit of Prato Cathedral (left) and a 'theatre for preaching' designed by Leonardo da Vinci with a central pulpit and semi-circular rising seats

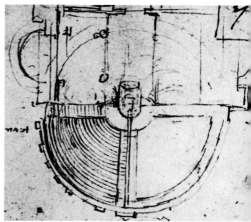

126, 127 Two famous preachers. Vincent Ferrer (right) and Giovanni Capestrano (far right) were both credited with large numbers of conversions – in Ferrer's case, Jews, Moors and heretics in Spain and France; in Capestrano's, Hussites in central Europe

christ was stopping up the mouths of Christ's true spokesmen, was a consistent belief of the Lollards. The right to preach the word of God without any form of prohibition or interference was likewise one of the four articles of the Hussite programme. Yet while Hus, Jerome of Prague, Savonarola and many lesser persons died at the stake for what they had preached as well as written, others arrived in the canons of Catholic saints for their ability as preachers.

It indicates the great respect for the spoken – as well as the written – word, that three Latin saints of the fifteenth century earned fame and canonization for their work as preachers. The Spanish Dominican, Vincent Ferrer, and the two Italian Franciscans, Giovanni Capestrano and Bernardino of Siena, all found enormous popularity during their lives and were canonized after their death for their tireless work as preachers. Vincent Ferrer, born in 1350 at Valencia, was nearing fifty when he began his full preaching career, and by the time he died, still preaching, in Brittany in 1419 he had won renown, according to Nicholas of Clémanges, as 'a man whom everyone talks of and praises,' not only in Spain but also in Provence, Piedmont, Savoy, Switzerland, Flanders and France. The huge audiences he attracted are the more remarkable in that he seems always to have spoken in his own vernacular, but such was the power of his oratory that he was said to have the gift of tongues. Capestrano's thirty years' activity as a preacher likewise took him to many parts of Europe. It ended climactically with his death, aged seventy, at Belgrade in 1456, after the victory over the Turks which he had helped to promote. His failure to speak German and Polish had not prevented him from undertaking an extensive preaching tour through the Empire in the 1450s. 'Such was his manner of speaking that even those who did not understand were moved to tears and amendment of life,' reported a German chronicler, who had received in Nuremberg a direct report of the preacher's drawn appearance and impressive speech.

Great preachers were great events. Though they might (as did Capestrano) have the help of an interpreter, it was the spectacle and the eloquence as much as the meaning which held vast audiences captive. But in the final count it was concern for understanding as well as for entertainment which attracted congregations – even at the hour of dawn – and which kept them through two, three or four hours' speaking. 'How could you believe in the holy sacrament of the altar, but for the preaching you have heard . . . and how, but for sermons, would you know what sin is?' San Bernardino asked one of his audiences. Believing so whole-heartedly in the value of understanding he was quite prepared to say that if it was necessary to choose between a Mass and a sermon 'you should let the mass go, rather than the sermon.' 'I give thanks to you for your patience,' he said to a congregation at Padua about a year before his death; 'you were never weary, but, on the contrary, came day after day, growing in number, fervour and zeal, harkening eagerly to the divine word.' San Bernardino's zeal was certainly untiring. By the time he was fifty-two – already toothless, emaciated and aged before his time, as contemporary depictions show him – he had been preaching almost daily for twenty-eight years. Such was his celebrity when he died in 1444 that he was canonized within six years, and in the second half of the century many buildings were dedicated to him, and decorated with the monogram of the name of Jesus which he had made so much his own.

Fifty years later, in a characteristic farewell sermon, another famous preacher told the Florentines, 'I have preached so often, and laboured so hard, as to have shortened my life by many years.' Savonarola's boast was less justified than one by Bernardino would have been – though his death-wish was shortly to be granted. Words certainly helped to shorten his life, but whereas Bernardino had shown how the pulpit could lead to sainthood, Savonarola showed how it could help political revolution. His oratory played an important part in the ejection of the Medici from Florence in 1494 and in the establishment of a republican government. Savonarola too, like San Bernardino (though with so different an outcome), had rejected a life of retreat for the activity of preaching. 'I was led from my own home to the port of religion. . . . at the age of twenty-three years in search of the two things most dear to me – liberty and quiet. But then I looked on the waters of this world, and by preaching I began to win a few souls.'

The Mass and the sermon show similar forces at work. Laymen were concerned with forms of religion which provided them with personal assurance and consolation, with a sense of direct spiritual contact. They found such certainty in ways which tended to diminish the role of ecclesiastics, of church institutions, even of the sacraments. 'God loves one soul more than all the churches in the world,' said San Bernardino. In this age of spiritual individualism many people might become more convinced of this fact by listening to a sermon than by attending Mass in church, and even the Mass could become an attribute of personal contemplation more than of corporate worship. While sermons could be a preferred alternative to attendance in church they might also take place outside it. The Hussites received the eucharist in the open air; others besides Italians listened to sermons out of doors. San Bernardino, who delivered one sermon from a tree, was one of the preachers who often held forth in market squares or open fields. 'All the land of Prato seemed turned into a church,' a biographer remarked of Savonarola's successes. For all the energy they put into it, preachers were unable to transform either church or world, but they contributed to the intensity of religious experience outside the walls of the church.

The late medieval struggle for spiritual revaluation also led to revulsion against things worldly in general, in both church and world. Puritanism had an important place in fifteenth-century piety. An exaggerated disgust for the extravagances of secular life and for corporal existence, the sense of the corruption of the flesh and of all things fleshly, appear in phrases and actions of people in all quarters across the century. 'Do not call me Highness, for I am only a sack of earth and worms,' said John II of Portugal at his death in 1495. The sentiment was shared by humble heretics as well as by an archbishop of Canterbury who looked forward to emancipation from 'this wretched putridity and carcass, my body.' 'Fetid, putrid, stinking': it is easy to see the inherent pessimism in such adjectives to which contemporary tomb sculpture gave vivid visual expression. Savonarola was not the only preacher of the century who fanned the emotions of his audiences into near-frenzies of self-denying enthusiasm. Bonfires of 'vanities' into which people threw playing-cards, dice, false hair, paintings and books were celebrated before his time and in other countries than Italy. There was indeed a morbid element in such demonstrations. Yet those whose sense of death is very acute may also have a full sense of life. The emphasis upon individual corruption was equalled by the strong awareness of Christ's humanity, to which San Bernardino called his listeners' attention as he held the sacred monogram before their eyes, and to which visionaries like St Catherine of Genoa so clearly witnessed. Although many contemporaries were deeply conscious of the doom of many of the externals of life, they could balance despair with optimism in the boundlessness of inner spiritual resources. Their belief was not weaker because it was introverted.

Like other ages whose institutions appeared to have been failing, the later Middle Ages produced a kind of *Schwärmerei*, an enthusiasm which was essentially introspective. Old ideals went on being

propounded and pursued but there were also new developments, and it is no accident that the most positive forms of religious experience and the most formative reorientations of thought took place in towns. It was in the activity of urban surroundings that San Bernardino and Savonarola attracted their largest audiences, that the *Devotio Moderna* radiated its influences, and that humanist philosophy was formed. It was in civic centres that the conflict between old and new ways was felt most acutely, and in such places emerged the most original contributions to new forms of belief.

'We have been mistaken,' Pius II reports himself as having said in overt chagrin at the opening of the Congress of Mantua in 1459, sadly surveying the paltry gathering which represented the response to his summons to the whole of Christendom. 'We have been mistaken. Christians are not so concerned about religion as we believed.' Perhaps he was doubly mistaken. The concern of the age was profound, but its ideas of religion were changing. Christians had great faith in the faith, but less confidence in the powers of the church.

The most fervent call to religion was no longer the call to retreat from the world or to answer the summons to ecclesiastical office. It was most intense where ideals of personal asceticism were combined with active secular existence, and the highest spiritual endeavours of this age were not so much those of monks and hermits, or of popes and bishops, but those of readers concentrating on their books, teachers instructing their pupils, preachers declaiming to their congregations. Christianity had become more self-critical, more introspective, at once more afraid and more confident in the face of worldly demands. Christians had acquired greater independence in relation to the ministrations of the church. People did not cease to believe but they were learning to believe in different ways, and while many of them were imitating Christ with the utmost fervour they found ways of doing so which did not always bring them into church. Churchmen had never been the whole of the church; society had always been demanding. It may be that religiosity and ecclesiasticism can never be wholly united. By the end of the Middle Ages they had grown perilously apart.

173

128 The cadaver of Cardinal Lagrange, from his tomb at Avignon. This was one of the first of such monuments, completed after his death in 1402

129, 130
Poliphilus,
the hero of
Francesco
Colonna's
*Hypneroto-
machia
Poliphili* (1499),
portrayed in
a landscape
with classical
ruins. Below, a
boy reading
Cicero

VI THE SENSE OF RENEWAL

Now, indeed, may every thoughtful spirit thank God that it has been permitted to him to be born in this new age, so full of hope and promise, which already rejoices in a greater army of nobly-gifted souls than the world has seen in the thousand years that have preceded it.

MATTEO PALMIERI, *On Civic Life* (1435-40)

Fabrizio praised the place as being delightful; and particularly considering the trees and failing to recognize some of them, remained in suspense. Perceiving this Cosimo said, 'perhaps you are not acquainted with some of these trees, but do not wonder at this, for some of them were more celebrated among the ancients than they commonly are today.'

MACHIAVELLI, *The Art of War* (1520)

Every period produces its own vocabulary. As Machiavelli remarked, 'whenever new ideas or new arts come to a place, new words necessarily come too.' New concepts demand new terms and old words acquire different overtones in changing circumstances. The fifteenth century produced much that was new, geographical, intellectual and artistic, and in the process of turning the language of the past to creative new efforts it generated a new terminology, of art and learning and history. It is a terminology which we still use and discuss. In the processes of history however – unlike the processes of science – words tend to be found after rather than before the understanding of the phenomena they stand for, and it was not until considerably later, by which time history had itself been transformed, that historians settled upon the word 'Renaissance' as a convenient if confusing shorthand for the great surge of activity and excited sense of renovation which animated that period in its attitude to the past. The idea was there long before the word. In literature and in art, in architecture and in religion, thinkers, writers, painters and planners from Petrarch and Boccaccio onwards were becoming   175 increasingly aware that they stood in a special relationship to the achievements of antiquity. Their obsession with this heritage of the past, and the uses they made of it, generated a historical reorientation unparalleled in any earlier period of classical revival. Out of their impassioned enthusiasm to recover the works of antiquity grew both the idea of a cultural interregnum – an age designated as dark or middle – and also an enlarged evaluation of the potentiality of the present. The dialogue of history was altered.

'For you', wrote Petrarch in 1338, a year after his first revelatory visit to Rome, apostrophizing the Latin epic *Africa* upon which, years before his death, contemporaries already hung his claim to fame, 'for you, if you should long outlive me, as my soul hopes and wishes, there is perhaps a better age in store; this slumber of forgetfulness will not last for ever. After the darkness has been dispelled, our grandsons will be able to walk back into the pure radiance of the past.' The wish was amply fulfilled. Petrarch's successors continued and extended his efforts to recover and communicate with the giants of antiquity. They became conscious of the disappearing darkness.

'Some of your works', the poet mournfully addressed Cicero in a letter, 'have (unless I am mistaken) undoubtedly been lost to us, who are now living, I do not know whether irreparably.' For Petrarch one of the most deplorable indictments of his generation was the loss of the works of Cicero – since boyhood the greatest love of his literary life. When in 1345 he experienced the great joy of discovering Cicero's letters to Atticus in the chapter library at Verona, he set to and transcribed them himself, although he was unwell. 'My great love and delight and the desire to possess the work overcame my physical infirmity and the labour of the task.' Some years later this same Cicero made Petrarch ill for nearly a year with a festering graze on his ankle, where the poet had repeatedly bumped into the volume on his way into his study. It was a cherished and personally appreciated wound, which caused him to take to his bed and even (which was saying a lot) to call in a doctor. With Greek antiquity, for all his admiration, the poet's exchanges were less intimate and less fruitful. The Homer which he received with unbounded delight from Constantinople in 1354 remained a closed book to him, despite his efforts to learn Greek, until 1367 when – after long waiting – he at last received a translation. Since, as he put it, fortune did not favour his study of Greek, Homer remained mute to Petrarch though Petrarch himself was far from mute, even if he was perforce deaf to this 'best of leaders'. In the long letter which he wrote to Homer he enumerated the handful of followers whom the Greek poet then had in several cities of Italy, and counselled him – though Petrarch himself did not always follow this advice – to hope for the best.

Petrarch, thus living and talking with his antique preceptors, heralded a new period of fruitful converse with the past. Yet for all his enormous admiration for these ancient heroes (Cicero, Seneca, Quintilian, Livy, Virgil, Homer) who dominated his poetic aspirations, there was an ambivalence in Petrarch's attitude – as perhaps there must be in all true understanding of the past. With his dual linguistic loyalties he was prophetic even where he was uncertain. He blamed Cicero even while he praised him; he lived with Homer, yet he sensed his absolute separation. The problem of reconciling past and present found him divided, seeming, as he put it, to find himself placed between two different peoples, looking simultaneously on that of the past and that of the future. Awed as he was by the superiority of the past, he found it necessary to excuse himself for not following ancient examples in writing about his own times; the trouble was, he explained, that his contemporaries seemed subjects for satire rather than for history. This ambivalence continued. The sense of inferiority before the greatness of the past was accompanied by a feeling of renewed creative possibilities in the present. The movement which we have come to know as the Renaissance was compounded both of diffidence in the face of antiquity and of confidence in the discovered abilities of the moderns.

'He restored to light this art which for many centuries had been buried under the errors of some who painted in order to please the eyes of the ignorant, rather than satisfy the intelligence of the experts.' Boccaccio's praise of Giotto, repeated and elaborated up to

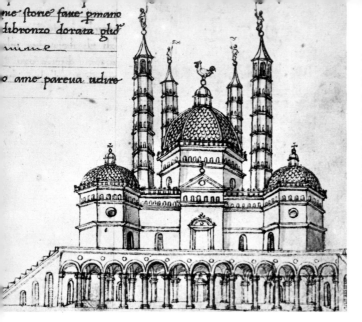

ne storie fanne primano
dibronzo dorata glo
mine

o anne parena udire

and beyond Vasari, became a keystone in the theory of revival. It was the idea of the revivified arts for which the words 'renaissance', 'rinascità' and 'Wiedererwachsung' were first employed in the sixteenth century. In architecture as well as in sculpture and painting it came to seem possible to re-enter the ancient world by contemplating the creations of the new. 'My lord, I seem to see again the noble buildings that were once in Rome and those that we read were in Egypt. It seems to me that I have been reborn on seeing those noble buildings.' Such were the words, put into the mouth of a lordly connoisseur as appreciation of the fictitious city of Sforzinda, by which the practising architect Antonio Filarete (c. 1400–69) hoped – in a treatise written in the 1460s – to convince a Milanese patron of the stylistic advances already visible in Florence. Antiquity could not only be recaptured; it could also be remade, and it was in Florence that the 'antique mode of building' first seemed to have been realized. Although painters – and acclaimers of painters – were ahead of builders, and the hopes and realizations of writers preceded both, the visual as well as the literary scene had been greatly changed by the middle of the century. There seemed to be plenty of grounds for optimism, and for the kind of propaganda that is born of confident persuasion. But Petrarch's ambivalence was still discernible

in Machiavelli. 'The world is the same as it was, the sun the same, the elements the same; virtue alone is diminished,' Petrarch had written, reminding the emperor Charles IV of the virtues of ancient Rome. The same pessimistic belief in moral decline appears in Machiavelli's contemplation of the ruin – above all the military ruin – of his over-invaded country, in lamentable contrast to the ways of 'true and perfect antiquity'.

Despite the continuance of pessimism, the better age for which Petrarch longed had, at least in some respects, arrived less than two generations after his death in 1374. Already by about 1430, thanks to the fervent researches of such men as Coluccio Salutati and Poggio Bracciolini, the corpus of writers recovered from antiquity was almost complete – though the searches were far from ended. In the first part of the fifteenth century those who wanted to learn Greek no longer suffered from the frustrations which Petrarch had experienced. It was possible to attend courses in a number of Italian cities besides Florence. Though facility in Latin greatly predominated over fluency in Greek, knowledge of both, as well as more writings in both, extended outside Italy. European scholars became more widely familiar with the works of antiquity, and the apologies which Petrarch had addressed to Cicero and Homer no longer applied.

Ideas like snow take time to settle. The recovery of texts proceeded, considering the circumstances, with remarkable rapidity once Poggio and others had communicated their enthusiasm, but the use which was made of them depended upon a change of outlook which was slower to establish itself. It was more than a question of recovering knowledge; it was also a matter of reception. Given fresh eyes, even known texts or known buildings could become the source of new inspiration, and it was new vision more than recovered works which produced advances. The work of Quintilian, for example, had been known continuously in a mutilated form when, in 1350, Petrarch was presented with an imperfect copy of the *Institutes of Oratory* which enabled him to perceive afresh Quintilian's great value for educational training, and to hope that the rest of the text might be recovered. It was not, however, until two generations later, after Poggio Bracciolini had discovered the full text of this work in the library of St Gallen, that understanding of the *Institutes* received practical expression. Quintilian's ideas of the purposes of education then became one of the foundations of the methods practised by great teachers such as Guarino da Verona at Ferrara, and Vittorino da Feltre in the renowned school which started when, in 1423, he went to teach the children of Gianfrancesco Gonzaga, marquis of Mantua. Philosophy and eloquence, mental and physical exercise, were to prepare each individual to develop his or her particular gifts for 'the life of social duty'. Classical studies were a way of life, a preparation and guide for the full being of the active citizen. This was the meaning of the *studia humanitatis*, and already about the middle of the fifteenth century those who applied themselves to these studies had (being dubbed after the manner of medieval scholastic slang) earned themselves the name of *umanista*, humanists.

In architecture the investigation of buildings went with the investigation of texts. Antiquity, then as now, was to be read on the ground as well as in books, and for the Florentine humanists who regained it antiquity was to be seen above all in the civic guise of Rome. The discovery of Rome, whose imposing ruins had long been an inspiration to those with a taste for the ancient past, went along with the literary recovery and, like it, was pursued more systematically than in earlier periods of such interest. Rome, its theatres, temples, altars, arches, palaces and columns, was not merely described and annotated. It was also measured and analysed so that it might – in more senses than one – be rebuilt. Besides Poggio Bracciolini and Flavio Biondo (1392–1463), who went so far beyond Petrarch in their investigations and descriptions of ancient monuments, the researchers included architects and designers, whose anxiety to discover the principles of construction and proportion exceeded the desire to learn the literary associations and correct identification of Roman buildings.

The lure of Rome was the lure of a visual treasury, particularly for those with known creative purposes. The two friends Filippo Brunelleschi (1377–1446) and Donatello (c. 1386–1466), who spent some time together in Rome early in the century, were so indefatigable in their excavations and examination of buried capitals, cornices and other remains, that they are reported to have earned themselves the name of 'the treasure-seekers'. For Brunelleschi – as for Bramante, who likewise went to Rome later in the century to measure ancient models as accurately as possible – the objective was essentially practical. Already he was brooding over the technical problems of the dome for the cathedral in Florence, for which purpose he specially studied the vaulting of the Pantheon.

134–138 Quintilian, representing rhetoric, on the choir stalls at Ulm (far left). Vittorino da Feltre (centre) had great influence as an educator, and his pupils included the son of another great teacher, Guarino da Verona (left). Vittorino taught Cecilia Conzaga to read the Gospels in Greek before she was eight; Pisanello's medal (right) shows her with a unicorn and the inscription 'Cicilia Virgo'

Meanwhile, one of the most original architects of the century, Leone Battista Alberti, convinced like Brunelleschi that to build well it was essential to understand the theory of Roman architecture, earned fame as much for his books as for his buildings. In his *Ten Books on Architecture* he aimed to do what Vitruvius had done for the Romans – to define the principles of harmony, beauty and ornament in building. It was in large measure a task of restoration. Vitruvius' work, like Quintilian's, had been known and copied through earlier centuries, and was revised after Poggio's visit to St Gallen. But Alberti's standards were those of observation and practice, and he had to reconstruct the relics of what he found. 'It grieved me that so many great and noble instructions of ancient authors should be lost by the injury of time, so that scarce any but Vitruvius has escaped this general wreck; a writer indeed of universal knowledge, but so maimed by age that . . . he might almost as well have never written at all, at least with regard to us, since we cannot understand him.' It was grievous also that so many surviving theatres and temples from which there was so much to be learnt were 'mouldering away daily' – though plenty of opportunities remained for supplementing literary with archaeological researches. Alberti approached his self-appointed task with exceptional eyes and exceptional energy. 'There was not the least remains of any ancient structure that had any merit in it, but what I went and examined, to see if anything was to be learned from it. Thus I was continually searching, considering, measuring and making drafts of everything I could hear of.' It was a great age for treasure-hunts in general – and they helped the making of measures.

To humanist historians, as to researching architects, the vital past reappeared – as it was seen to have flourished and disappeared – in the shape of a city. Humanist history written on this understanding introduced a new periodization. Instead of the past being viewed as a continuous process of decline leading from the Roman empire to ultimate dissolution in the reign of Antichrist, it became a dynamic process of the prosperity, decay and restoration of republican virtues. Here, as in so many other places, Petrarch had shown the way by regarding the fall of the Roman empire as a dividing-point between 'ancient' and 'modern' history, and by alluding to the Christian barbarian period after it as a time of darkness. Variously expanded and elaborated upon by later historians, this concept introduced a new way of dividing history, in which the period of Roman greatness was seen to be separated from the period of contemporary recovery by an intermediate age of obscurity. The first historians to formulate this interpretation differed in their chronological framework. Leonardo Bruni (1374–1444), in the twelve books of his *History of the Florentine People*, thought that decline had begun with Roman imperial despotism and that revival started with the gradual emergence of the Italian communes after the *imperium* had been removed to Germany in the ninth century. Flavio Biondo, on the other hand, whose *Decades of History from the Decline of the Roman Empire* were written slightly later (1439–52), considered that the barbarian invasions, in particular the sack of Rome by the Goths early in the fifth century, marked the real beginning of decay. This event was followed by a thousand years, to which he devoted attention as a period of special obscurity, which intervened before the beginning of contemporary history. In their different ways Bruni and Biondo set a new pattern for historical periodization by suggesting this concept of a break between antiquity and modern times. The idea of a 'middle age' lying between decline and revival was created.

The humanists were a great deal more than antiquarian collectors. They were concerned to use the past as well as to regain it. The classical heritage was freshly investigated and become freshly meaningful because it was capable of being re-created. It was the leading model for modern works. But these two aims – the recovery of the past and the realization of the present – were not wholly compatible, and understanding of the discrepancy between them helped to improve the quality of contemporary creations and the consciousness of modern style. The sense of the unlimited possibilities of going forward had to be preceded by an awareness of the limitations of going back. The very comprehensiveness of the efforts to rationalize the classical heritage for modern use promoted a better appreciation of the qualities of fifteenth-century modernity. And what we have inherited from the Renaissance is a new estimate of the new as well as a wider knowledge of the old.

The concern to utilize antiquity led to the formulation of rules, and these rules themselves came to be regarded as marking the advance of the moderns. New languages need new grammars, in painting and building as much as in writing and composing. The fifteenth century produced guides in all these fields. What Alberti and Filarete did for painting and architecture others did in other spheres; they aimed to codify the principles of antique excellence to improve the work of contemporaries and successors. It was necessary to know the principles of building as a science, Filarete asserted in his treatise on architecture, and the antique way of doing things was more commendable and beautiful than the modern in part for the very reason that it had 'better rules'. Alberti, whose treatise *On Painting* (1435) contained the first theoretical exposition of the principles of perspective – which had already been demonstrated in practice by Brunelleschi and Masaccio – wanted to establish the necessity for painters to know the mathematical laws of spatial diminution. 'The best artist,' he wrote, 'can only be one who has learned to understand the outline of the plane and all its qualities.'

139 A manuscript of Valla's *Elegantiae* with an initial showing the author at work. Valla extolled the excellence of ancient languages, especially Latin

140, 141 Leone Battista Alberti (above) owed much in his writings to the work of contemporary artists. Masaccio's *Holy Trinity* (right) was one of the earliest paintings to demonstrate the theory of perspective which Alberti shortly afterwards expounded

The work which became an indispensable handbook for literary composition was Lorenzo Valla's *Elegantiae linguae latinae* (1444), which established stylistic criteria by a systematic analysis of Latin forms. Meanwhile Alberti pointed the way to the future by being the first to produce an Italian grammar which demonstrated that the vernacular was governed by comparable rules and could itself be regarded as comparable to the Latin from which it was descended. Treatises also appeared which explained the proportions of letters of the alphabet. The humanists of the fifteenth century were responsible for both the Italic and Roman hands in use today, and also – somewhat later in the century – for bringing Roman capital letters back into use. Respect for what they thought of as the 'antiqua littera' of earlier medieval manuscripts, led Petrarch, Salutati, Poggio,

185

Niccolo Niccoli (1363–1437) and others to experiment with new hands and to modify their Gothic scripts by imitating Carolingian models. Out of these experiments arrived the new forms which were later adopted by the printers. Among those who, about the middle of the century, helped to restore the correct form of Roman capital letters was the painter Andrea Mantegna (1431–1506), who was interested in inscriptions as well as in Roman architecture and costume. Roman lettering, just as much as buildings and sculpture, could be regarded as manifesting classical perfection of form. In the second half of the century works were written to explain the principles of geometrical construction of the letters of the Roman alphabet.

What began as a literary and artistic movement was capable in the end of reshaping politics and society. The belief that the experience of classical Rome was vitally relevant for the recuperation of contemporary Italy stirred many Italians between Petrarch and Machiavelli. Many changes, though, took place between the republican experiment of the Roman tribune Cola di Rienzo in 1347 and the writing of Machiavelli's *Discourses* early in the sixteenth century. Rome's topography was altered as well as understanding of its past. It came to be seen in politics, as elsewhere, that the knowledge of antiquity must be applied in a freshly assimilated form, not simply by reference to particular examples.

The clearest statement of this advance of thought was given by Machiavelli. In both his *Art of War* (completed in 1520) and in his *Discourses* (of the previous decade) he was absorbed by the same problem: to reduce Roman experience – above all Roman military experience – to its elements for the improvement of his own age. 'I answer you again, that the ancients did all things better and with greater prudence than us; and, if we make mistakes in other things, in the affairs of war we do everything wrong,' he wrote. To discover the principles behind the success of the Romans was to discover the source of present remedies. Italy had declined because it had neglected the military practices of antiquity (especially by employing mercenaries and by neglecting the virtues of infantry), and though modern warfare differed from that of ancient Rome, particularly in the use of artillery, the general principles remained the same. They

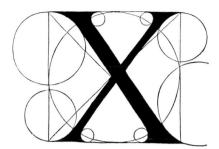

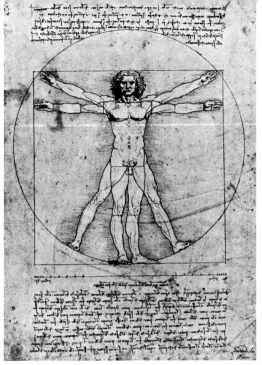

142, 143 *De Divina proportione* (1509) by the mathematician Luca Pacioli, in which this letter appears, was completed in 1497. Illustrations for it were provided by Leonardo da Vinci, the author's close friend and associate. Leonardo's own intensive study of human proportions, including the drawing on the right, may have been stimulated by Pacioli

should still be applied. 'My intention,' said Machiavelli near the end of the *Art of War*, 'has not been to show just how ancient warfare was conducted, but how in these days a form of war might be ordained which should have more virtue than the one which is used.' The purpose of his *Discourses* was similar. They formed a commentary upon the chapters and books of Livy's first decade, investigating the Roman constitution and empire and the example of the great men of Rome, for the purpose of assisting modern government. Machiavelli, like earlier searchers of ancient texts and monuments, was grieved by the losses of the past. He also lamented, and was specially concerned to remedy, the 'lack of a proper appreciation of history' in his predecessors, above all – as he saw it – their failure to see beyond particulars to valuable generalized principles. In history, as much as in law or medicine, general prescriptions could be induced from particular instances. The lessons of history, like the lessons of war, were reducible to rule.

The demonstration that war and politics, painting, building and writing were scientific activities, based upon definable principles, was derived in each case from belief in the superiority of ancient example.

187

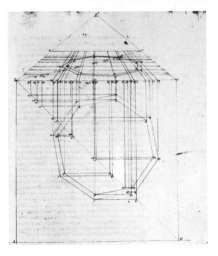

144, 145 Piero della Francesca worked out with great care the architectural planning and spatial relationships of *The Flagellation of Christ* (far right). He must have drawn the ground-plan as if for a real building, according to the method described in his *De Prospettiva pingendi*, which contains the study (right) of the perspective of an inlaid pavement

In each case what emerged was a greater sense of the autonomy of these activities in the present. The very procedures adopted by the humanists in this great burst of enthusiasm set them apart from their classical preceptors, as they themselves came to realize. They had to recognize what the ancients had lacked as well as what they had possessed. The admission added to the pride of contemporary achievement. Explorers were proud.

It is easy at this distance to see that the buildings of Brunelleschi and Alberti and the paintings of Masaccio and Mantegna are original precisely because they were so much more than imitations. They fused what had been learnt from antiquity with new knowledge and existing traditions. The awareness that this was so, the understanding that their problems and their world were different in kind from the reverenced world of Rome, had already arrived in the fifteenth century. It enhanced the humanists' consciousness that they were making a new world, one which had already produced good works and which could go on to produce better. They began to see the past as finite, the future as infinite.

Alberti and Machiavelli were both conscious of undertaking new enterprises, of doing something which had never been done before. Machiavelli compared his researches into politics to the dangerous daring of those who 'set off in search of new seas and unknown lands'. The exploit was perilous but exciting, and if there were rewards they lay essentially in the future, with those who would follow these new,

previously untrodden ways. Alberti also regarded himself as a pioneer. In explaining the theory of painting and the mathematical laws of perspective he was embarking, he thought, upon 'a subject never before treated'. The undertaking enabled him to feel that the genius of the moderns surpassed that of the ancients who had probably never reached this knowledge, and whose position was in any case so much easier since they had so many more models to imitate. Even Lorenzo Ghiberti, who believed that the rules of artificial perspective had been formulated in antiquity, had to admit that if this was the case they had been lost. His discussion of this matter, like that of Piero della Francesca, was derived as much from medieval writers on optics as from knowledge of antiquity. However much some of the humanists might deplore the decline which had followed the fall of Rome and the barbarism of the medieval centuries, they could not ignore that heritage. The novelty of their position lay in the ways in which they borrowed and welded as well as in the ways in which they disavowed.

'If he can make a handsome mixture of the noble orders of the ancients, with any of the new inventions of the moderns, he may deserve commendation,' said Alberti of the intending architect. To combine well was to create well, and Alberti put his advice into practice in his own designs and buildings. His plans for Santa Maria Novella in Florence and for the Malatesta Temple in Rimini demonstrated – for all his careful attention to the orders of Roman buildings – how the application of old forms to modern structures could produce completely new results. A Roman triumphal arch could not be grafted on to the front of an aisled church without giving rise to technical problems which called for inventive solutions. As Alberti himself recognized, innovation deserved acclaim just as much as renovation. The architectural work which contemporaries – Florentines in particular – looked upon as one of the chief wonders of their day was glorious precisely because it surpassed the glories of the Romans. The new Rome could vie with the old. Brunelleschi's dome, triumphantly dominating the city of Florence, symbolized the achievement.

> Who [asked Alberti] could ever be hard or envious enough to fail to praise Pippo the architect on seeing here such a large structure, rising above the skies, ample to cover with its shadow all the Tuscan people, and constructed without the aid of centering or great quantity of wood? Since this work seems impossible of execution in our time, if I judge rightly, it was probably unknown and unthought of among the ancients.

146, 147 The reconstruction which was to turn the church of San Francesco, Rimini (left), into a temple for Sigismondo Malatesta, began in 1447. It was never completed but a commemorative medal of 1450 shows the temple as Alberti must have planned it

148 The great achievement of Renaissance engineering admired by Alberti and Michelangelo. Brunelleschi's dome of Florence Cathedral (above) was built without centering and completed, apart from the lantern, when he died in 1446

Brunelleschi roused wonder and admiration by inventing a new method of vaulting without the elaborate scaffolding which was assumed to be needed. But his design made use of both Roman and Gothic elements and in fact achieved precisely that mixture of old and new which Alberti advocated. Exactly the same process of fusion formed new styles in other fields – in the new scripts which also combined Carolingian and Roman with remaining Gothic elements, and in literature where the vernaculars gained from the digested understanding of classical Latinity.

To view the past with Alberti's creative vision was to see it as essentially dynamic. The discovery of the principles of ancient excellence meant the discovery of the principles of perfectibility. The idea that the more that was known about the past the better the future might be was inherent in humanist activities from Petrarch onwards. 'Nothing is at the same time both new born and perfect,' wrote Alberti. 'I believe that if my successor is more studious and more capable than I he will be able to make painting absolute and perfect.' It was more than a formal profession of modesty. Grief at the losses of the past did not exclude hopes for the future. Machiavelli thought it blameworthy in rulers not only to fail to profit from the knowledge of antiquity but also to 'have not an inkling of the future'. Albrecht Dürer, like Alberti (and for the same reasons), looked to a future when his own works would happily be surpassed, and when art would attain greater excellence. 'Many notable men' would arise who would make fresh discoveries so that 'the art of painting may in time advance and reach its perfection.'

If the future was potentially expansive the present was recognizably so. Its very inventiveness drew attention to its intrinsic originality, and the discoveries of the time were considered and acclaimed in the context of history. Technical inventions as well as mental dexterity constituted a gulf between antiquity and its imitators, and the idea that 'no man without invention was ever excellent in his skill' was present before Machiavelli and Leonardo da Vinci agreed in propounding it. The fifteenth century possessed tools, techniques and knowledge which, had they been present in antiquity, might (it seemed) have changed the course of ancient history. There was the discovery of gunpowder and artillery which had introduced new problems into the conduct of war so that even Machiavelli, though he denied that the elements of warfare were any different, had to admit that as an offensive weapon it would have added to the speed of Roman conquest. 'If any man could have discovered the utmost powers of the cannon . . . and have given such a secret to the Romans, with what rapidity would they have conquered every country and have vanquished every army,' wrote Leonardo. There were lesser inventions which were also praiseworthy, such as the coloured terracottas made by the Della Robbias which Leonardo valued particularly because they seemed to him to give painting a durability which was comparable to sculpture. And, of course, there was the great discovery of printing which made Gutenberg seems as generative as Ceres, Mainz like the Trojan horse, the modern age a new age of gold.

Contemporaries were able to rejoice in discoveries which revealed the uniqueness of the generation which had conceived them. Increasingly conscious of the autonomy of their own time they also endowed the activities they were pursuing with a more autonomous standing. Politics and art began to find more independence, to be differently related to society. Theories of government and artistic theories were both revolutionized in the Renaissance. The naked exposition of political facts which gave such notoriety to Machiavelli's *Prince* marked the arrival of the idea of government as an autonomous secular activity, capable of making its own morality, capable of being considered apart from Christendom. Neo-Platonic thought and the theory of perspective helped to produce a comparable revolution in art. The rules of perspective were more than a procedure for correctness; they were also a formula for perfection. They were concerned with the interpretation of space, as well as with its representation and the problems involved in translating three dimensions into two. The laws of proportion could be applied in other spheres than painting, and a church or temple as much as a picture could reveal to the viewer, through its metrical order, the symphonic harmony of the universe. The Neo-Platonic ideas expressed in the elaborate symbolism of Piero della Francesca's

'Flagellation', and the carefully harmonized structure of Brunelleschi's Church of San Lorenzo in Florence, brought art and religion into a new relationship. The Gothic church also had its principles of mathematical proportion, but they were directed towards a more purely sacramental form of religious experience. Churches by Alberti, Bramante and later Palladio, like paintings by Botticelli and Piero della Francesca, were themselves expressions of divine harmony and forms of spiritual revelation. Visual symbols and artistic representation became invested with a new content, and the relationship between the religious and the aesthetic was altered. Art, as an activity which could be spiritual without being ecclesiastical, could find a new standing in secular society – and so could artists. It was the beginning of a whole new aesthetic.

If there was any single theme linking together the various activities which have come to be designated by the term 'Renaissance', it was a passionate interest in the inheritance of the ancient past, a concern which included history. It began essentially with attachment to the qualities of antiquity but it extended into better understanding of the whole historical process, and of the relationship of present with past and future. The whole of the past may be potential history, but none of it can be properly understood without a sense of the irrevocability, as well as the heritability, of what has happened. Many roads have taken admirers to the Roman past, but it was the humanists of the fifteenth century who opened the way which has led furthest and the one which we still – if tacitly – follow. It was not only that they were more convinced, more numerous and more conscientious than those who had preceded them. It was also because they became more realistically aware of the limitations and possibilities of their connections with classical antiquity. The more they learnt of it the more they became aware both of themselves and of their own age. They became more discerning and more practised in the uses they tried to make of antiquity. Through exploring and imitating and analysing the works of the past they discovered how to appreciate better the potentialities of what was new. What emerged was a critical sense of period and style as well as a sense of the antique.

The results were ultimately momentous in religion, as in art and literature.

The ability to evaluate the qualitative differences of different periods was generally absent from medieval historical thought. Petrarch's wish to restore the textual accuracy of Livy, and his letters addressed to Livy and Cicero dated by 'the birth of that God whom you never knew', show the beginnings of a consciousness of historical separation which grew with the work of later humanists. Antiquity, Salutati pointed out, must be judged by standards different from our own. If justice were really to be done to Virgil or Aeneas it was necessary to get back to a world of pre-Christian values, as he himself tried to do in defending Virgil against a charge of having dishonoured Augustus' lineage by making Aeneas the illegitimate son of a mortal (Anchises) and a goddess (Venus) – the misunderstanding of a world which had different ideas of divinity, matrimony and legitimacy. To understand the past it was necessary to enter imaginatively into a whole realm of differences, inner and outer, of thought, assumption, appearance, behaviour – and language. It was something which Ciceronian writers and classicist painters both took time to realize.

The enthusiasm of some of the new-style admirers of antiquity was such that they attempted to write of their own times with the terminology and stylistic equipment of Sallust or Livy. Not unnaturally the results were hardly convincing, though this did not prevent their recruiting admirers. Bernardo Rucellai (1448–1514) modelled his account of the invasion of Florence in 1494 by Charles VIII of France so closely on Sallust that he omitted all reference to one of the chief actors in those events – Savonarola. Erasmus passed the dubious compliment of describing this work as having the appearance of being 'written by another Sallust or certainly in the time of Sallust.' Such procedures were understandably inhibiting, for to see modern events through ancient eyes (using ancient words) entailed failing to see a good many things which might be important to contemporaries – including ecclesiastical and miraculous occurrences. Another member of Rucellai's intellectual circle wrote astringently of those 'who want to trace everything back to antiquity

149 Mantegna's arch-
aeological researches
are evident in his
*Trial of St James
before Herod Agrip-
pina.* The triumphal
arch is authentically
Roman and the
costumes are depicted
according to antique
patterns

and silently pass over many things that have been changed or completely innovated since then,' and Flavio Biondo commented on the problems of trying to stretch the linguistic equipment of the Romans to cover an age which had artillery, and other instruments of war unparalleled in antiquity. Expecting an ass to run like a horse was how Guicciardini castigated the blind classicism of some contemporaries. It was no good, he pointed out, trying to quote the Romans in all circumstances. To do so it would have been necessary to reproduce a city with exactly the same conditions as theirs. Their qualities were different. The times had moved forward. The innovations of the new age demanded their own terminology, as Alberti and Ghiberti discovered when they began to write on art and had to invent words.

If it was misleading to omit any mention of Savonarola in an account of Florence in the 1490s, it was no less distorting to depict within an elaborately reconstructed 'antique' setting two figures doing duty for Paris and Helen, attired in the most fashionable garments of contemporary Burgundian costume. There were contemporary critics who understood and commented also upon these anomalies, and who were learning to appreciate all the elements of gesture, expression, manner and costume which characterize persons and periods.

When you make a figure of a man who has lived in our own times, he should not be dressed in the antique fashion but as he was. What would it look like if you wanted to portray the duke of Milan and dressed him in clothes that he did not wear? It would not look well and it would not look like him. It would be the same to make the figure of Caesar or Hannibal and make them timid and dress them in the clothes that we wear

150, 151 Donatello was criticized because he used his knowledge of ancient armour to invest Gattamelata (below) with the military prowess of antiquity. But the Florentine artist who, in about 1460, drew the abduction of Helen, made the figures almost indistinguishable from fashionable Burgundian courtiers, in striking contrast to the antique setting in which he placed them

today . . . they should be done according to their quality and their nature.

The author of these remarks, Antonio Filarete, made a significant contribution to the theories already being developed by Alberti and others, by seeing so clearly that an understanding of historical proprieties formed an integral part of the laws of harmony which were seen to determine beauty. Alberti had explained that all animate beings conform to definable rules of gesture and movement. Filarete pointed out that individuals must be seen to conform not only to themselves, but also to their times. Disrespect for the present was as bad as disrespect for the past. Every age should be accorded its own qualities. He rebuked severely those who failed to observe this rule: Donatello for the inappropriate costume of his Gattamelata; Masolino for having painted past saints in modern clothing.

Exactitude may sometimes seem to be the enemy of art. Not surprisingly many contemporary artists continued to neglect these new canons. Yet there certainly were painters who tried to observe such strictures. Mantegna, for instance, made careful investigations in order to represent correctly the costume of the Roman legionaries, as well as the architectural setting, in his legend of St James. The association of style with historical understanding was, in general, an important development of the Renaissance concern for the past. It proved to be highly significant in matters of religion.

Despite the essential historicity of Christianity, perceptive understanding of the historical figure of Christ was far from common in the Middle Ages – for all the efforts which were made – and religious practices in various ways militated against it. Religious transcendentalism, the doctrine of transubstantiation, and belief in the repeated sacrifice of the Mass all tended – especially among the unsophisticated – to obscure realization of the fact that Christ's life and death were completed historical events which had taken place more than fourteen hundred years earlier. Art may in some ways have contributed to the lack of historical clarity. The Christian story was presented to contemporaries with all the vivid actuality of

152 Christ in a contemporary setting. Conrad Witz's *Miraculous Draught of Fishes* was commissioned by the bishop of Geneva and shows the landscape of the Lake of Geneva in the background

their own world – with the buildings, landscapes, costumes and countenances with which they were familiar. Indeed in certain respects the increased realism of fifteenth-century painting heightened the contemporaneousness of Biblical representations. An altarpiece by Conrad Witz (d. *c.* 1446), for instance, painted for the cathedral of Geneva, enabled the inhabitants of the city to see Christ walking on the waves of their own lake, with a group of Apostles like their own local fishermen, set against the familiar and accurately depicted landscape of Mont Salève and the distant range of Mont Blanc. Savonarola, though he believed in the value of religious art when used properly, took Florentine painters to task for the dangerous profanity of their over-realistic presentation of contemporary models. 'The young men,' he complained, 'go saying of this figure and that figure, this is the Magdalen, and that is Saint John. For you cause the figures to be painted in the churches in the likeness of this or that woman, which is wrongly done, and in great contempt of the things of God.' It was a sign of the new times that painters were thus conceiving their saints through observing individuals, rather than through following conceptualized models.

199

Although it is true that the mystical always cuts across the historical experience, there were elements of danger for religion in the lack of historical clarity. 'Jesus is long since dead,' a priest pointed out to Margery Kempe when she fell into one of her fits of tearful religiosity after contemplating a *pietà* in a church in Norwich. 'Sir,' Margery replied to him, rebukingly, 'his death is as fresh to me as if he had died this same day, and so methinketh, it ought to be to you and to all Christian people.' In a sense she was right, of course. Yet such approaches were capable of producing unorthodox attitudes – and not only among the illiterate. Over-concentration upon the Passion and sufferings of Christ and the Virgin, which became so conspicuous in the later Middle Ages, gave rise to the idea of a 'perpetual Passion' in which Christ was regarded as still suffering for the injuries which mankind was still inflicting upon him. This concept appears in a Dürer woodcut of 1511 in which the resurrected Christ, bearing the insignia of the Passion, is shown suffering the mockery of a sneering soldier. The contemporary nature of the wound is emphasized by an attached verse which includes the words, 'I still take floggings for thy guilty acts.'

An awareness of the differences of different periods of the church's past characterized movements for religious change long before the Reformation. One of the main ingredients of heresy of many different kinds was to raise the banner of 'primitivism' (the standards of the early church being used as the criterion for judging modern corruptions) in the name of reform and return. The enlarged historical perspectives of the fifteenth century contributed enormously to the effectiveness of such approaches. Here as elsewhere fresh concentration upon sources brought revolutionary change – in this case through the application of historical criticism to the textual bases of belief, including the Bible.

Lorenzo Valla (1407–57) showed that new methods could be dynamite when applied ruthlessly to medieval tradition. In 1440 he wrote a shattering *exposé* of the Donation of Constantine – the eighth-century document which purported to contain the transference of imperial privileges to the church by the Emperor Constantine in the fourth century. The Donation had long had critics, but not until the fifteenth century was it dealt with in such a way that it was conclusively established to be a forgery. It is significant of the extension of new critical approaches that two other individuals reached the same conclusion as Valla by similar procedures. Nicholas of Cusa in the 1430s and Reginald Pecock about 1450 also decided that the Donation was apocryphal, though their onslaught was less thorough than Valla's. His work, written in propagandist circumstances and in a highly polemical vein, pressed the case against the Donation to the point where it could gain general acceptance. He went beyond Cusa and Pecock in applying historical criticism to the text to show that it could be discredited by its own terminology. It was, as he demonstrated, riddled with anachronisms. 'Do the Caesars speak thus? Are Roman decrees usually drafted thus? Who ever heard of satraps being mentioned in the councils of the Romans?' Valla's case was born of new assurance, and the forging of the tools he used so effectively had begun with Petrarch.

The shock to established belief was greater when such methods were turned on to the Bible. Valla did this too. His *Annotations on the New Testament* (which Erasmus used and edited) boldly made use of philological criticism to examine and emend the text. Although he was careful to avoid the appearance of casting doubt upon the faith of scripture, he maintained that the Vulgate was open to correction – a belief which could only horrify many contemporaries. Comparison with the original Greek, which Valla carried out chapter by chapter, with the help of other sources (such as Homer), showed how many improvements could be made to the New

153 Dürer's woodcut of
The Man of Sorrows,
frontispiece to his Large Passion,
a mystical rather than
a historical representation

Testament text, on grounds of elegance as well as grammatical accuracy. Valla, being Valla, did not hesitate to make suggestions. The Bible for him was not an immutable mystery, an unalterable document inherited from unquestionable authorities. It was a historical text like other texts and, as a translation, open to philological analysis as much as any other work. 'I prefer to see with my own eyes, rather than with the eyes of others.' It was the affirmation of a period which had increased the belief in individuals and individual judgment, as well as in texts and textual studies.

Christ and the Apostles were also individuals, to be fitted into their particular circumstances in Roman history. When John Colet returned home from Italy in 1496, impressed by the achievements of the Italian humanists, he delivered some revolutionary lectures in the university of Oxford on the Epistles of St Paul. They were revolutionary precisely because they were concerned with that theme. The Apostles had to be considered as they themselves had acted, 'taking account of persons, places and times.' They were individuals as much as any of us – given their right place and freed from the deadening weight of scholastic tradition. Colet, turning to Suetonius in order to understand what the society of St Paul was really like, was engaged on a task like that of Mantegna, examining classical monuments before he painted St James. Here too historical approaches brought a new sense of reality. And they led others besides Erasmus to that most perplexing of all problems – the regeneration of the church.

In the process of recovering an old vocabulary the fifteenth century created a new one. By the end of the century fuller knowledge and practical experience had increased understanding and changed the ways of looking at classical antiquity. It was not only that people had learnt to see that the past was qualitatively different from their own age, and irrecoverable. It was also the sense that the moderns were more than dwarfs peering out from the shoulders of giants; they might in some ways be inferior, but their own works were worthy of acclamation. They did not merely imitate, they used old models to invent new creations. The sense of renovation penetrated literature and politics and religion, but it was early and most clearly evident in the arts. These provided the physical emblems of modernity, and the Renaissance itself, like the New World, was a visible phenomenon before it arrived as an intellectual concept with a name. Already in the fifteenth century, long before Giorgio Vasari and others gave it wider currency, the idea had begun to be expressed that the artistic achievements of the time deserved comparison with antiquity, and that new light was dawning after a regrettable intermediate period of darkness. The idea of the Renaissance was essentially a contemporary idea about the very process of history. It was a time when, as a contemporary expressed it, minds became more subtle and reawakened to the past.

Of course there was still darkness. Old forms of thought and old fears, old superstitions and old hesitancies continued through the fifteenth century and far beyond. But what was new was as important as what was old, and to some it seemed more striking. We shall do contemporaries an injustice if we do not recognize the feeling of renewal as well as the feeling of doom with which their age was pervaded. They had a sense of delight and also a sense of damnation. Both deserve recognition.

History being what it is, no age can ever be taken entirely at its own estimation. Yet it cannot be taken without it either. It is arguable that we have allowed ourselves to remain dominated too long by the concept of themselves, of their time and history, which the thinkers and writers of the Renaissance so triumphantly asserted. They had an assurance in the past as well as a concern for the present to buttress the novelty of their periodization. We, with our longer perspectives, have lost many of their certainties and uncertainties and have gained others. The Dark Ages have lost much of their darkness, and the Middle Ages of their middleness. If we choose to go on viewing that part of the past in a light which derives from the great reorientation of the fifteenth century, one of the reasons must be that it succeeded in making a world in which we can still feel relatively at home. The 'Middle Ages' were conceived at the very moment when they were thought to be passing away. It was the beginning of modernity, the making of the Renaissance.

SELECT BIBLIOGRAPHY

This list is necessarily very selective, and is confined to works in English and to translations of sources cited in the text.

I GENERAL WORKS

BURCKHARDT, J. *The Civilization of the Renaissance in Italy* (London 1878)
Cambridge Economic History of Europe, vol. II (Cambridge 1952)
Cambridge Medieval History, vol. VII, *Decline of Empire and Papacy*, vol. VIII, *The Close of the Middle Ages* (Cambridge 1932–6)
CHASTEL, A. *The Age of Humanism. Europe 1480–1530* (New York 1954; London 1963)
CHEYNEY, E. P. *The Dawn of a New Era, 1250–1453* (New York 1936)
FERGUSON, W. K. *Europe in Transition, 1300–1520* (London 1962)
GILMORE, M. P. *The World of Humanism, 1453–1517* (New York 1952)
HAY, D. *Europe in the Fourteenth and Fifteenth Centuries* (London 1966)
HUIZINGA, J. *The Waning of the Middle Ages* (London 1937)
New Cambridge Modern History, vol. I, *The Renaissance, 1493–1520* (Cambridge 1957)
PARRY, J. H. *The Age of Reconnaissance* (London 1963)
THOMPSON, J. W. *Economic and Social History of Europe in the Later Middle Ages* (New York 1931)

II SOURCES IN TRANSLATION

Advocates of Reform, From Wyclif to Erasmus, ed. M. Spinka (Philadelphia and London 1953)
ALBERTI, L. B. *On Painting*, ed. John R. Spencer (London 1956)
    Ten Books on Architecture, trans. C. Bartoli and J. Leoni (London 1955)
BOCCACCIO, GIOVANNI *The Decameron*
Bondage and Travels of Johann Schiltberger, a Native of Bavaria, in Europe, Asia and Africa, 1396–1427, ed. J. Buchan Telfer (Hakluyt Society, London 1879)
Book of Margery Kempe, 1436, a modern version by W. Butler Bowden (London 1936)
Canon Pietro Casola's Pilgrimage to Jerusalem in the Year 1494, ed. M. M. Newett (Manchester 1907)
CASTIGLIONE, BALDESAR *The Book of the Courtier*, trans. C. S. Singleton (New York 1959)
Council of Constance. The Unification of the Church, trans. L. R. Loomis, ed. J. H. Mundy and K. M. Woody (New York and London 1961)
De Orbo Novo. The Eight Decades of Peter Martyr D'Anghera, trans. F. A. MacNutt, 2 vols (New York and London 1912)
ERASMUS *The Adages*, ed. M. M. Phillips (Cambridge 1964)
    Handbook of the militant christian, trans. J. P. Dolan (Indiana 1962)
    The Praise of Folly, trans. H. H. Hudson (Princeton and London 1941)
FABRI, FELIX *Wanderings in the Holy Land*, ed. Aubrey Stewart, 2 vols (Palestine Pilgrims' Text Society, London 1892–3)

Filarete's Treatise on Architecture, trans. and ed. John R. Spencer (New Haven and London 1965)

GUICCIARDINI, FRANCESCO *History of Italy and History of Florence*, trans. C. Grayson, ed. and abridged J. R. Hale (New York 1964)

Selected Writings, ed. C. Grayson, trans. M. Grayson (Oxford 1965)

HUS, JOHN *The Church*, trans. and ed. David S. Schaff (New York 1915)

The Letters of John Hus, ed. H. B. Workman and R. M. Pope (London 1904)

John Hus at the Council of Constance, trans. and ed. M. Spinka (New York and London 1965)

Journal of Christopher Columbus, trans. C. Jane, revised L. A. Vigneras (London 1960)

À KEMPIS, THOMAS *The Imitation of Christ*

Literary Works of Leonardo da Vinci, ed. J. P. Richter and I. A. Richter, 2 vols (Oxford 1939)

MACHIAVELLI *The Art of War*, revised edition of the Ellis Farneworth Translation, intro. by Neal Wood (Indianapolis 1965)

The Discourses, trans. L. J. Walker (London 1950)

History of Florence and of the Affairs of Italy, intro. F. Gilbert (New York 1960)

The Literary Works, trans. and ed. J. R. Hale (Oxford 1961)

Mandeville's Travels. Texts and translations, ed. M. Letts, 2 vols (Hakluyt Society, London 1953)

Memoires of Philip de Commines, ed. A. R. Scoble, 2 vols (London 1855–6)

Narrative of the Embassy of Ruy Gonzalez de Clavijo to the Court of Timur at Samarcand, AD 1403–6, ed. C. R. Markham (Hakluyt Society, London 1859)

NICHOLAS OF CUSA *Of Learned Ignorance*, trans. G. Heron, intro. by D. J. B. Hawkins (London 1954)

Unity and Reform, Selected Writings of Nicholas de Cusa, ed. J. P. Dolan (Chicago 1962)

Pero Tafur, Travels and Adventures, 1435–39, trans. and ed. M. Letts (London 1926)

PETRARCH *Letters to Classical Authors*, trans. M. E. Cosenza (Chicago 1910)

Letters from Petrarch, selected and ed. Morris Bishop (Indiana 1966)

Life of Solitude, ed. J. Zeitlin (Urbana 1924)

Secret, ed. W. H. Draper (London 1911)

Pilgrimage of Arnold von Harff, trans. and ed. M. Letts (Hakluyt Society, London 1946)

PIUS II *Commentaries*, trans. and ed. F. A. Gragg and L. C. Gabel (Smith College Studies in History, vols XXII, XXV, XXXV, XLIII, Northampton, Mass. 1937–57)

Memoirs of a Renaissance Pope, trans. F. A. Gragg, ed. L. C. Gabel (London 1958). (An abridgement of the *Commentaries*)

Renaissance Philosophy of Man, ed. E. Cassirer, P. O. Kristeller and J. H. Randall (Chicago 1948)

Saint Catherine of Siena as seen in her Letters, trans. and ed. V. D. Scudder (London and New York 1905)

SAVONAROLA *The Triumph of the Cross*, trans. J. Proctor (London 1901)

Select Documents illustrating the Four Voyages of Columbus, trans. and ed. C. Jane, 2 vols (Hakluyt Society, London 1930–2)

Ship of Fools by Sebastian Brant, trans. E. H. Zeydel (New York 1944)

Travels of Bertrandon de la Brocquière, ed. T. Wright (London 1848)

Travels of Leo of Rozmital, 1465–67, trans. and ed. M. Letts (Hakluyt Society, Cambridge 1957)

Treatise of Lorenzo Valla on the Donation of Constantine, trans. C. B. Coleman (New Haven 1922)

VASARI, GIORGIO *The Lives of the Painters, Sculptors, and Architects*, ed. William Gaunt, 4 vols (London 1963)

Vespasiano Memoirs, trans. W. G. and E. Waters (London 1926)
Writings of Albrecht Dürer, trans. W. M. Conway (London 1948)

III SECONDARY WORKS

ADY, C. M. *Pius II (Æneas Silvius Piccolomini), the Humanist Pope* (London 1913)
ATIYA, A. S. *The Crusade in the Later Middle Ages* (London 1938)
BARON, H. *The Crisis of the Early Italian Renaissance* (Princeton 1955, revised edition 1966)
   'Cicero and the Roman Civic Spirit in the Middle Ages and Early Renaissance', *Bulletin of the John Rylands Library*, XXII (1938), pp. 72–97
   'Franciscan Poverty and Civic Wealth as Factors in the Rise of Humanistic Thoughts', *Speculum*, XIII (1938), pp. 1–37
BARRACLOUGH, G. *The Origins of Modern Germany* (Oxford 1949)
BENESCH, O. *The Art of the Renaissance in Northern Europe* (Cambridge, Mass. 1945)
BLUNT, A. *Artistic Theory in Italy, 1450–1600* (Oxford 1940)
BRILIOTH, Y. T. *Eucharistic Faith & Practice* (London 1930)
BROCK, P. *The Political and Social Doctrines of the Unity of Czech Brethren* ('s Gravenhage 1957)
BÜHLER, G. F. *The Fifteenth-Century Book. The Scribes, the Printers, the Decorators* (Philadelphia 1960)
BUSH, D. *Prefaces to Renaissance Literature* (Cambridge, Mass. 1965)
CALMETTE, J. *The Golden Age of Burgundy* (London 1962)
CARTELLIERI, O. *The Court of Burgundy* (London 1929)
CASSIRER, E. *The Individual and the Cosmos in Renaissance Philosophy* (Oxford 1963)
CHABOD, F. *Machiavelli and the Renaissance* (London 1958)
CLARK, JAMES M. *The Dance of Death in the Middle Ages and the Renaissance* (Glasgow 1950)
CLARK, KENNETH *Leonardo da Vinci* (Harmondsworth 1958)
COHN, N. *The Pursuit of the Millennium* (London 1957)
CONNOLLY, J. L. *John Gerson, Reformer and Mystic* (Louvain 1928)
COULTON, G. G. *Five Centuries of Religion*, vol. IV, *The Last Days of Medieval Monachism* (Cambridge 1950)
CREIGHTON, M. *History of the Papacy from the Great Schism to the Sack of Rome*, 6 vols (London 1897)
DANNENFELDT, K. H. *The Renaissance: Medieval or Modern?* (Boston 1959)
DAWSON, C. *Medieval Essays* (London 1953)
Europe in the Late Middle Ages, ed. J. R. Hale, J. R. L. Highfield and B. Smalley (London 1965)
FERGUSON, W. K. *Renaissance Studies* (London, Ontario 1963)
   The Renaissance in Historical Thought (Boston 1948)
FITZGERALD, V. *Saint John Capistran* (London 1911)
FLICK, A. C. *The Decline of the Medieval Church*, 2 vols (London 1930)
GARIN, E. *Italian Humanism. Philosophy and Civic Life in the Renaissance* (Oxford 1965)
GEANAKOPLOS, D. J. *Greek Scholars in Venice* (Cambridge, Mass. 1962)
GILBERT, F. *Guicciardini and Machiavelli; politics and history in early sixteenth-century Florence* (Princeton 1965)
GILL, JOSEPH *The Council of Florence* (Cambridge 1959)
GILMORE, M. P. *Humanists and Jurists; Six Studies in the Renaissance* (Cambridge, Mass. 1963)
GOLDSCHMIDT, E. P. *Medieval Texts and Their First Appearance in Print* (London 1943)

GOMBRICH, E. H. *Norm and Form: Studies in the Art of the Renaissance* (London 1966)
The Story of Art (London 1966)
GREEN, V. H. H. *Bishop Reginald Pecock; a Study in Ecclesiastical History and Thought* (Cambridge 1945)
HALE, J. R. *Machiavelli and Renaissance Italy* (London 1961)
HARVEY, J. H. *The Gothic World, 1100–1600; a Survey of Architecture and Art* (London 1950)
HAY, D. *Europe, The Emergence of an Idea* (Edinburgh 1957)
The Italian Renaissance in its Historical Background (Cambridge 1961)
The Renaissance (London, B.B.C., 1963)
HEARNSHAW, F. J. C. *The Social & Political Ideas of some great thinkers of the Renaissance and the Reformation* (London 1949)
HEYMANN, F. G. *John Žižka and the Hussite Revolution* (Princeton 1955)
HÜGEL, F. VON *The Mystical Element of Religion as Studied in Saint Catherine of Genoa and her Friends*, 2 vols (London 1909)
HUIZINGA, J. *Erasmus of Rotterdam* (London 1924)
HYMA, A. *The Christian Renaissance; A History of the 'Devotio Moderna'* (Grand Rapids 1924, Hamden, Connecticut 1965)
Italian Renaissance Studies, ed. E. F. Jacob (London 1960)
JACOB, E. F. *Essays in the Conciliar Epoch* (Manchester 1953)
JAYNE, S. R. *John Colet and Marsilio Ficino* (Oxford 1963)
JONES, RUFUS M. *The Flowering of Mysticism* (New York 1939)
KRISTELLER, P. O. *The Classics and Renaissance Thought* (Cambridge, Mass. 1955)
Eight Philosophers of the Italian Renaissance (Stanford 1965)
The Philosophy of Marsilio Ficino (New York 1943)
LEA, H. C. *A History of the Inquisition of the Middle Ages*, 3 vols (London 1906)
LECLER, J. *Toleration and the Reformation*, vol. 1 (London 1960)
LEFF, G. *Heresy in the Later Middle Ages. The Relation of Heterodoxy to Dissent c. 1250–1450*, 2 vols (Manchester 1966)
MCFARLANE, K. B. *John Wycliffe and the Beginnings of English Nonconformity* (London 1952)
'The Wars of the Roses', *Proceedings of the British Academy*, L (1965), pp. 87–119
MANNING, B. L. *The People's Faith in the Time of Wyclif* (Cambridge 1919)
MATTINGLY, G. *Renaissance Diplomacy* (London 1955)
MEISS, M. *Painting in Florence and Siena after the Black Death* (Princeton 1951)
MITCHELL, R. J. *The Laurels and the Tiara; Pope Pius II, 1458–64* (London 1962)
MOMMSEN, T. E. 'Petrarch's Conception of the Dark Ages', *Speculum*, XVII (1942), pp. 226–42
MORISON, S. E. *Admiral of the Ocean Sea; a Life of Christopher Columbus* (Boston 1942)
MORRALL, J. B. *Gerson and the Great Schism* (Manchester 1960)
ODLOŽOLÍK, O. *The Hussite King; Bohemia in European Affairs, 1440–1471* (New Brunswick 1965)
Wycliffe and Bohemia (Prague 1937)
ORIGO, I. *The Merchant of Prato: The Life and Papers of Francesco di Marco Datini* (London 1957)
The World of San Bernardino (London 1963)
'The Domestic Enemy: the Eastern Slaves in Tuscany in the Fourteenth and Fifteenth Centuries', *Speculum*, XXX (1955), pp. 321–66
PANOFSKY, E. *Renaissance and Renascences in Western Art* (Copenhagen 1960)
The Life and Art of Albrecht Dürer (Princeton 1955)
PARKER, G. H. W. *The Morning Star. Wycliffe and the Dawn of the Reformation* (Exeter 1965)

PARKS, G. B. *The English Traveler to Italy*, vol. 1 (Rome 1954)

PASTOR, L. VON *The History of the Popes, from the close of the Middle Ages* (London 1891–1953), vols 1–6 ed. S. I. Antrobus

PEARS, E. *The Destruction of the Greek Empire and the Story of the Capture of Constantinople by the Turks* (London 1903)

PENROSE, B. *Travel and Discovery in the Renaissance, 1420–1620* (Cambridge, Mass. 1952)

PERNOUD, R. *Joan of Arc, by herself and her witnesses* (New York 1966)

PERROY, E. *The Hundred Years War* (London 1951)

PETRY, R. C. *Late Medieval Mysticism* (London 1947)

PRESTAGE, E. *The Portuguese Pioneers* (London 1933)

PUTNAM, G. H. *Books and their Makers during the Middle Ages*, 2 vols (New York and London 1896–7)

RASHDALL, H. *The Universities of Europe in the Middle Ages*, ed. F. M. Powicke and A. B. Emden, 3 vols (Oxford 1936)

Renaissance Debate, ed. D. Hay (New York, etc. 1965)

RIDOLFI, R. *The Life of Niccolò Machiavelli* (Chicago 1963)
The Life of Girolamo Savonarola (London 1959)

ROBB, N. A. *Neoplatonism of the Italian Renaissance* (London 1935)

ROOVER, R. DE *The Rise and Decline of the Medici Bank* (Cambridge, Mass. 1963)

RUNCIMAN, S. *The Fall of Constantinople 1453* (Cambridge 1965)

RUSSELL, J. C. *Late Ancient and Medieval Population* (American Philosophical Society, Philadelphia 1958)

SEEBOHM, F. *The Oxford Reformers* (London 1887)

SEIDLMAYER, M. *Currents of Medieval Thought with special reference to Germany* (Oxford 1960)

SELLERY, G. C. *The Renaissance, Its Nature and Origins* (Madison 1950)

SOUTHERN, R. W. *Western Ideas of Islam in the Middle Ages* (Cambridge, Mass. 1962)

SPINKA, M. *John Hus' Concept of the Church* (Princeton 1966)

SPITZ, L. W. *The Religious Renaissance of the German Humanists* (Cambridge, Mass. 1963)

STEINBERG, S. H. *Five Hundred Years of Printing* (Harmondsworth 1955)

SYMONDS, J. A. *The Renaissance in Italy*, 7 vols (London 1875–98)

THORNDIKE, L. *Science and Thought in the Fifteenth Century* (New York 1929, 1963)

TIERNEY, B. *Foundations of the Conciliar Theory* (Cambridge 1955)

ULLMAN, B. L. *The Humanism of Coluccio Salutati* (Padua 1963)
The Origin and Development of Humanistic Script (Rome 1960)

ULLMANN, W. *The Origins of the Great Schism* (London 1948)

VAUGHAN, D. M. *Europe and the Turk: A Pattern of Alliances, 1350–1700* (Liverpool 1954)

WATANABE, M. *The Political Ideas of Nicholas of Cusa* (Geneva 1963)

WEISS, R. *Humanism in England During the Fifteenth Century* (Oxford 1941, 1957)
The Spread of Italian Humanism (London 1964)

WHITFIELD, J. H. *Petrarch and the Renaissance* (Oxford 1943)

WILKINS, E. H. *Life of Petrarch* (Chicago 1961)

WINSHIP, G. P. *Printing in the Fifteenth Century* (Philadelphia 1940)

WITTKOWER, R. *Architectural Principles in the Age of Humanism* (London 1949)

WOODWARD, W. H. *Studies in Education during the Age of the Renaissance, 1400–1600* (Cambridge 1906)
Vittorino da Feltre and Other Humanist Educators (Cambridge 1897)

NOTES ON THE ILLUSTRATIONS

1 Detail of painting showing the conquest of Trebizond by the Turks, on a cassone from the Strozzi Palace, Florence; c. 1475. The Metropolitan Museum of Art, New York (Kennedy Fund, 1913)

2 Woodcut world map, from Hartmann Schedel's Liber chronicarum; Nuremberg, 1493

3 Map showing Turkish conquest. Drawn by Shalom Schotten

4 Miniature showing payment of the ransom of the Count of Nevers to Bajezid I, from Froissart's Chronicles; the ransom, fixed at 200,000 ducats for all the captured leaders, eventually totalled much more. French, 15th C. MS Harl. 4380, fol. 118r. Courtesy Trustees of the British Museum, London

5 Coloured woodcut of the Battle of Zonchio; the victorious Turkish commander was Kemal Ali (shown as 'Chmali' in the background); the commanders of both Venetian ships shown in the foreground, Andrea Loredano (left, Nave Lordana) and Albano Armer (right, Nave del Armer), were lost. Venetian, c. 1499. Courtesy Trustees of the British Museum, London

6 Portrait of Mohammed II by a Turkish artist; 15th C. Topkapi Museum, Istanbul

7 Map of Constantinople by Cristoforo Buondelmonte, from his Isolario; 1420. MS lat. 4285, fol. 37r. Bibliothèque Nationale, Paris

8 Death taking the printers and bookseller, woodcut from La grant danse macabre; Lyons, 1499

9 The Triumph of Death, from a series of engravings of Petrarch's Trionfi; Venetian, c. 1470–80 British Museum, London. Photo: John Freeman

10 The dead man and his Judge, miniature from the Grandes Heures de Rohan; the Lord is God the Father and Christ in one. French, early 15th C MS lat. 9471, fol. 159r. Bibliothèque Nationale, Paris

11 Procession of flagellants, marginal drawing attributed to the Limbourg brothers from a Book of Hours; 1407. MS Douce 144, fol. 110r. Courtesy Curators of the Bodleian Library, Oxford

12 Map showing the course of the plague in western Europe. Drawn by Shalom Schotten

13 Woodcut sheet with the martyrdom of St Sebastian and a prayer against the plague; German, 1437 (one of the earliest dated woodcuts). Osterreichische Nationalbibliothek, Vienna

14 Schematic view of Genoa, woodcut from the Supplementum chronicarum; Venice, 1486

15 The building of the Temple, miniature by Jean Fouquet from Antiquités judaïques; c. 1470. The Temple is in the form of a French late Gothic cathedral; a treadwheel crane is shown over the portal, and in the foreground workmen are dressing stone, carving statues, carrying water and mixing cement. MS fr. 347, fol. 163r. Bibliothèque Nationale, Paris

16 View of Cologne, detail of the Arrival of St Ursula, from the Shrine of St Ursula by Memling; 1489. Musée de l'Hôpital St-Jean, Bruges. Photo: R. Van de Walle

17 Map of the territories of the duchy of Burgundy. Drawn by Shalom Schotten

18 Detail of the Ile de la Cité in Paris, from the Descent of the Holy Ghost, miniature by Jean Fouquet; mid-15th C. The Lehman Collection, New York

19 Detail of a Flemish town, from the St Joseph wing of the Mérode Altarpiece by the Master of Flémalle (Robert Campin); c. 1425-8. The Metropolitan Museum of Art, New York (The Cloisters Collection, Purchase, 1957)

20 Drawing of the Colosseum by Silvestro da Ravenna, from the Codex Escurialensis (fol. 24v); c. 1480. Escorial Library. From H. Egger, Codex Escurialensis, 1906

21 Platina received as Vatican Librarian by Sixtus IV, by Melozzo da Forlì; 1477. Vatican Galleries. Photo: Archivio Fotografico Gallerie e Musei Vaticani

22 View of Naples (the 'Tavola Strozzi'), by an unknown Italian artist; 1464 or 1479. Museo di S. Martino, Naples. Photo: Scala

23 Detail of woodcut view of Venice from Bernhard von Breydenbach's Sanctae peregrinationes; Mainz, 1486

24 Panorama of Florence by an unknown Italian artist; c. 1495. Private Collection, London

25 Detail of woodcut panorama of Antwerp; Flemish School, 1515. Cabinet des Estampes, Antwerp

26 Abbeville: detail of façade (north door) of St Wulfran; 1488-1539. Photo: Courtauld Institute of Art, University of London

27 Prague: interior of Vladislav Hall in the Castle, by Benedict Ried; 1493, rebuilt 1502-3 after collapse of the vault. Photo: Helga Schmidt-Glassner

28 Miniature showing Simon Nockart presenting a copy of the Chroniques de Hainaut by Jacques de Guise to Philip the Good; also present, besides Charles the Bold, are Jean Chevrot, bishop of Tournai (second from left), Chancellor Rolin (third from left), and Philip's natural son Anthony, Grand Bâtard de Bourgogne, a tall figure in black in the group of Knights of the Golden Fleece; Flemish, 1448. MS 9242, fol. 1r. Bibliothèque Royale de Belgique, Brussels

29 Cracow: courtyard of the Collegium Maius, showing the Jagiellonian Library; rebuilt in 1498 after a fire. Photo: J. Krieger

209

30 University lecture, from a drawing of the imaginary tomb of a professor by Jacopo Bellini. Louvre, Paris

31 Map showing universities in Europe founded before 1500. Drawn by Shalom Schotten

32 Centre panel of the *St Vincent Altarpiece* by Nuno Gonçalves; c. 1460. Museu Nacional de Arte Antiga, Lisbon. Photo: Abreu Nunes

33 Plan of the Sagres Promontory of Portugal, drawn by a member of Sir Francis Drake's party during the occupation of Sagres Bay, in May 1587. MS Cotton Aug.I.ii.113. Courtesy Trustees of the British Museum, London

34 World map of Henricus Martellus Germanus, from his *Insularium*; done at Florence, after 1489. MS Add.15760, fols. 68v–69r. Courtesy Trustees of the British Museum, London

35 Engraving of a ship in full sail; Venetian, late 15th C. British Museum, London. Photo: John Freeman

36 *The English Ambassadors taking Leave*, from a series of paintings by Carpaccio illustrating the legend of St Ursula; end 15th C. Accademia, Venice. Photo: Scala

37 *Reception of a Venetian Embassy in Cairo*; School of Gentile Bellini, probably late 15th C., though it has been suggested that this shows the embassy of Domenico Trevisan in 1512. Louvre, Paris. Photo: Mansell-Alinari

38 Bourges: courtyard of the house of Jacques Coeur; mid-15th C. Photo: ND

39 Drawing by Dürer of a pass in the Alps, thought to be in the Valle d'Isarco near Chiusa; 1495. Escorial

40 Portrait of Louis XI; School of Jean Fouquet, c. 1480. The Brooklyn Museum, New York

41 Detail of portrait of Maximilian I by Dürer; 1519. Kunsthistorisches Museum, Vienna

42 Portrait of Bianca Maria Sforza by Ambrogio de' Predis; probably 1493. National Gallery of Art, Washington, D.C. (Widener Collection)

43 Medal of Guicciardini; Bolognese, c. 1529. British Museum, London. Photo: John Webb (Brompton Studio)

44 Terracotta bust of Machiavelli; Italian, perhaps a pastiche in the style of the 16th C. Palazzo Vecchio, Florence. Photo: Mansell Collection

45 Silhouette of a female Negro slave; Italian, 15th C. Galleria Estense, Modena

46 Detail of medal of Cosimo de' Medici; Italian, mid-15th C. Bibliothèque Nationale, Paris. Photo: Jean Roubier

47 Drawing by Filarete of the Medici Bank in Milan, designed by Michelozzo, about the time of its completion; c. 1460. Biblioteca Nazionale Centrale, Florence

48 Detail of miniature showing Joan of Arc at the stake, from the *Vigils of Charles VII*; French, 1484. MS fr. 5054, fol. 71. Bibliothèque Nationale, Paris. Photo: Bulloz

49 Miniature from Pope Sixtus IV's copy of Guillaume Fichet's *Rhetoric*, showing Fichet presenting his book to the pope; several presentation copies, with dedication letters, were printed on vellum and illuminated; Paris, 1471. Courtesy Trustees of the British Museum, London

50 Printed list of books for sale at the inn 'Zum Wilden Mann', probably in Nuremberg, issued by the printer Peter Schöffer of Mainz; 1469/70. Bayerische Staatsbibliothek, Munich

51 Detail of one column from the 42-line Bible printed by Gutenberg; Mainz, ?1455.

52 Detail from a MS of Cicero's *De Oratore* copied by Poggio Bracciolini for Pope Martin V; 1428. Plut.50.31. Biblioteca Laurenziana, Florence

53 Detail from the first Italian edition of Cicero's *De Oratore*; Subiaco (Sweynheim and Pannartz), ?1465. British Museum, London. Photo: R.B. Fleming

54 *Battle of the Sea-Gods*, engraving by Mantegna; c. 1490. Albertina, Vienna

55 *Battle of the Sea-Gods*, copy by Dürer of the Mantegna engraving; 1494. Albertina, Vienna

56 Detail from the MS of Livy's *Ab Urbe condita* copied and annotated by Petrarch; c. 1330. Petrarch's library contained at the time a unique number of Latin texts, and also – though he could not read them – Plato and Homer in Greek. MS Harl. 2493, fol. 220v. Courtesy Trustees of the British Museum, London

57 Portrait of Humphrey, duke of Gloucester, from the *Recueil d'Arras*; mid-16th-C. copy by Jacques Leboucq of a 15th-C. original. Bibliothèque Municipale, Arras. Photo: Giraudon

58 Sketch portrait of Pirckheimer by Dürer; 1503. Kupferstichkabinett, Berlin

59 Ownership note by Humphrey, duke of Gloucester, from a Latin translation of the theological treatises of St Athanasius; before 1446. The note states: 'Cest livre est a moy homfrey duc de gloucestre le quel Jay fait translater de grec en latyn par Antoyne de Becaria Veroneys mon serviteur'. MS Royal 5.F.II, fol. 91v. Courtesy Trustees of the British Museum, London

60 Marginal drawing of a tournament of cupids, attributed to Dürer, from Pirckheimer's copy of the works of Aristotle edited and printed by Aldus Manutius in Venice, where Pirckheimer bought it in 1497. Museum Boymans-Van Beuningen, Rotterdam

61 Urbino: interior of the studiolo of Federigo da Montefeltro, in the Palazzo Ducale, with marquetry executed by Baccio Pontelli to designs perhaps by Botticelli; 1476. Photo: Scala

62 Detail of woodcut world map by Martin Waldseemüller, showing the New World, 'America'; 1507. From J. Fischer and F. von Wieser, *Die älteste Karte mit dem Namen America...*, 1903

63 *St George and the Dragon* by Raphael; 1504–6. National Gallery of Art, Washington, D.C. (Andrew Mellon Collection)

64 Urbino: courtyard of the Palazzo Ducale; begun 1447, enlarged and altered by Luciano Laurana after *c.* 1467. Photo: Mansell-Anderson

65 Portrait of Federigo da Montefeltro by Piero della Francesca; *c.* 1472. The duke lost his right eye in a tournament, which accounts for the peculiarity of his profile and the fact that he is never shown full-face. Uffizi, Florence. Photo: Alinari

66, 67 Session of the Council of Constance in the cathedral in November 1414, and mobile bakery (selling pretzels, among other things), from a MS version of Ulrich Richental's *Chronicle*; 1465. Rosgarten Museum, Constance

68 Nicholas of Cusa, from his funerary monument; *c.* 1500. S. Pietro in Vincoli, Rome. Photo: Mansell-Anderson

69 Detail of world map by Juan de la Cosa; 1500 Museo Naval, Madrid. Photo: Luis Dorado

70 Detail of map of central Europe attributed to Nicholas of Cusa; engraved at Eichstätt in 1491, this was the first print to be made from a copper plate. Courtesy Trustees of the British Museum, London

71 Drawing of the Parthenon, copy by Giuliano da Sangallo of a lost original by Ciriaco d'Ancona; from the *Codex Barberinianus*, late 15th C. Ciriaco's drawing was almost certainly fairly accurate, but this copy is 'Romanized': the Doric columns have Composite capitals though still – correctly – no bases, the metopes are placed above the pediment, and the whole building is raised on a plinth decorated with reliefs from the frieze. From C. Hülsen, *Il Libro di Antonio Sangallo*, 1910

72 Sketch of Manuel Chrysoloras by an unknown Italian artist; early 15th C. Louvre, Paris

73 *Two Venetian Ladies on a Balcony*, by Carpaccio; end 15th C. The painting has been cut down, and its original subject is unknown. Museo Correr, Venice. Photo: Marzari

74 Drawing by Dürer of ladies of Venice and Nuremberg; 1495. Städelsches Kunstinstitut, Frankfurt

75 Medal of the emperor John VIII Paleologus by Pisanello; the first Renaissance bronze medal, made on the occasion of the emperor's visit to Italy in 1438. Bibliothèque Nationale, Paris

76 Pilgrims returning from Compostella, marginal illumination from the *Hours of the Duchess of Burgundy*; French, 15th C. MS 76, fol. 9r. Musée Condé, Chantilly, Photo: Giraudon

77 Schematic woodcut of Jerusalem from Schedel's *Liber chronicarum*; Nuremberg, 1493

78 Woodcut title page from the 1515 edition of *Information for Pilgrims unto the Holy Land*; the work appeared in 1498. From the facsimile, ed. E.G.Duff, 1893

79 Pope Innocent VIII holding the tip of the Holy Lance, from his monument by Pollaiuolo; *c.* 1494-8. Bajezid hoped by this present to ingratiate himself with the pope, gaoler of his dangerous younger brother Djem who had been a hostage in the west for ten years; Bajezid tried to have Djem poisoned, and hoped for the pope's co-operation. St Peter's, Rome. Photo: Mansell Collection

80 End of bronze reliquary of St Zenobius by Ghiberti; 1434-42. Florence Cathedral. Photo: Mansell-Alinari

81 Pius II receiving the head-reliquary of St Andrew, from his funeral monument; *c.* 1464. Originally in Old St Peter's, Rome, the monuments of the Piccolomini popes were later moved to S. Andrea della Valle. Photo: Mansell-Anderson

82 Detail of the *Miracle of the Relic of the True Cross* by Carpaccio; *c.* 1494, one of a series painted for the Scuola di S. Giovanni Evangelista in Venice, which had possessed the relic since 1369. Accademia, Venice. Photo: Scala

83 Detail of page from the first Bohemian printed Bible, with coloured woodcut showing St Matthew writing his Gospel; 1489. British Museum, London. Photo: John Freeman

84 Supposed portrait of Sebastian Brant by Hans Burgkmair; 1508. Kunsthalle, Karlsruhe

85 Miniature portrait of a Turkish artist by Gentile Bellini; 1479-80. Isabella Stewart Gardner Museum, Boston

86 Baptism of the Moors of Granada, from the reredos of the Chapel Royal, Granada Cathedral, by Felipe Bigarny; *c.* 1522. Under the policies of Cardinal Ximenes, Granada was declared a Christian kingdom in 1502, Muslims being forced to convert or leave Spain. Photo: YAN

87 Medal of Pico della Mirandola by Niccolo Fiorentino; *c.* 1495. Courtesy Trustees of the British Museum, London

88, 89 Reverse and obverse of medal of Marsilio Ficino, attributed to Niccolo Fiorentino; before 1500. British Museum, London. Photo: John Webb (Brompton Studio)

90 *Pius II at Ancona*, fresco by Pinturicchio from a series begun in 1502. Piccolomini Library, Siena Cathedral. Photo: Mansell-Alinari

91 Detail of page from a German translation of *De duobus amantibus* (*Eurialis and Lucretia*) by Aeneas Silvius Piccolomini, later Pope Pius II; Strasbourg, 1477. British Museum, London. Photo: John Freeman

92 Savonarola preaching, woodcut from his *Compendio di revelatione*; Florence, 1495

93 Schoolroom from a Basel schoolmaster (?Myconius)'s hanging sign attributed to Ambrosius Holbein; 1516. Offentliche Kunstsammlung, Basel

94 *A Lecture at the Court of Urbino*, attributed to Justus van Ghent and to Pedro Berruguete; 1470s. Hampton Court. Reproduced by gracious permission of Her Majesty the Queen

95 Miniature showing John Colet kneeling before St Matthew, from a Bible containing both the

Vulgate and Erasmus' Latin translation; 1509. MS Dd. VII.3, fol. 6r. University Library, Cambridge

96 Roundel portrait of Erasmus by Hans Holbein the Younger; c. 1532. Öffentliche Kunstsammlung, Basel

97 Effigy of Pope John XXIII, from his monument by Donatello; 1425–7. Baptistery, Florence. Photo: Brogi

98 Silver-gilt chalice, from Avila; second half of the 15th C. H. 9.5 in. (24 cm.). Victoria and Albert Museum, London (Crown Copyright)

99 Prague: façade of the Týn Church; towers finished c. 1400. Photo: Helga Schmidt-Glassner

100 Hus led to execution, detail of coloured woodcut from Ulrich Richental's Chronicle; Augsburg, 1483

101 Pen drawing of a Hussite wagon-fortress; c. 1450. From H. Toman, Husitské válečnictví..., 1898

102 Allegorical engraving of the struggle between Pope Paul II and the emperor Frederick III; Venetian, c. 1470. British Museum, London. Photo: John Freeman

103 Tomb of Martin V, by Donatello; 1433. St John Lateran, Rome. Photo: Mansell-Alinari

104 Effigy of Leonardo Bruni, from his monument by Bernardo Rossellino; mid-15th C. Sta Croce, Florence. Photo: Mansell-Alinari

105 Portrait of Giuliano de' Medici by Botticelli; c. 1478. The open door and turtledove are symbols of death and mourning: they may either refer to the death of Giuliano's beloved Simonetta Vespucci in 1476 or – in which case the portrait is a posthumous copy – to the death of Giuliano himself in the Pazzi conspiracy of 1478. National Gallery of Art, Washington, D.C. (Samuel H. Kress Collection)

106 Terracotta bust of Lorenzo de' Medici by Verrocchio; c. 1485. National Gallery of Art, Washington, D.C. (Samuel H. Kress Collection)

107 Reverse of medal by Bertoldo di Giovanni commemorating the Pazzi conspiracy, showing the assassination of Giuliano de' Medici, below his head in profile; 1478. British Museum, London. Photo: John Webb (Brompton Studio)

108 Hanged men, from a page of studies by Pisanello; c. 1435. British Museum, London

109 Detail of miniature for January from the Très Riches Heures du duc de Berry, showing the duke at table, protected from the large fireplace behind him by a circular wicker screen; the wall in the background is hung with a tapestry of knights in battle; by the Limbourg brothers, 1413–16. MS 65, fol. 1v. Musée Condé, Chântilly. Photo: Giraudon

110 Detail of miniature for February from the Très Riches Heures du duc de Berry; by the Limbourg brothers, 1413–16. MS 65, fol. 2v. Musée Condé, Chantilly. Photo: Giraudon

111, 112, 113 Miniatures by Jean Bourdichon showing three of the four states of society; c. 1490. Collection Jean Masson, Ecole des Beaux-Arts, Paris. Photo: Giraudon

114 The Sermon in the Piazza del Campo by Sano di Pietro; mid-15th C. Opera del Duomo, Siena

115 Marble bust of Matteo Palmieri by Antonio Rossellino, displayed over the door of Palmieri's house in Florence until the 19th C.; 1468. Museo Nazionale, Florence. Photo: Mansell-Alinari

116 Reverse of medal of Savonarola, showing the Divine Punishment threatening the city of Florence; School of Della Robbia, 1497. British Museum, London. Photo John Webb (Brompton Studio)

117 Portrait of Savonarola by Fra Bartolommeo; 1490s. Museo S. Marco, Florence. Photo: Mansell-Alinari

118 Winchester: chantry chapel of Bishop William Waynflete, d. 1486, in the retrochoir of the cathedral. Photo: F.H.Crossley

119 Belem: interior of the church of the Jeronimos monastery; founded in 1499 by King Manuel with the proceeds of the voyages of discovery, and built in the early 16th C. Photo: Helga Schmidt-Glassner

120 The Blood of the Redeemer by Carpaccio; 1496. Museo Civico, Udine. Photo: Mansell-Fiorentini

121 Silver-gilt monstrance, from Perpignan; 15th C. Parish Church, Rigarda (Pyrénées-Orientales). Photo: Archives Photographiques

122 Sakramentshaus of limestone by Adam Krafft, in St Lorenz, Nuremberg; 1493–6

123 Detail of the Crucifixion from the Isenheim Altarpiece by Grünewald; c. 1515. The Altarpiece was painted for a hospital for incurables maintained by the Hermits of St Anthony at Isenheim in the Vosges, and Christ is shown suffering from the fatal disease treated there; Grünewald based the scheme of the Crucifixion on the 14th-C. revelations of St Bridget of Sweden. Musée Unterlinden, Colmar

124 Prato: outdoor pulpit of marble and bronze, on the cathedral, built to display the Virgin's girdle on certain festivals, and also used for preaching; by Michelozzo, Donatello, and others, 1428–38. Photo: Mansell-Alinari

125 Drawing by Leonardo da Vinci of a church choir arranged as a theatre for preaching, on the model of a classical amphitheatre; c. 1487. MS B, fol. 52. Institut de France, Paris. Photo: Courtauld Institute of Art, University of London

126 St Vincent Ferrer, from an altarpiece by Giovanni Bellini; c. 1465. SS. Giovanni e Paolo, Venice. Photo: Mansell-Alinari

127 Portrait of S. Giovanni Capestrano by Thoman Burgkmair; painted in memory of the saint's visit to Augsburg in 1452, when his preaching led to a bonfire of vanities witnessed by the eight-year old Thoman. National Gallery, Prague

128 Stone effigy of Cardinal Jean de Lagrange *en transi*, formerly at the bottom of an elaborate tomb which included, above, the marble effigy of the cardinal in his robes; *c.* 1402. Musée Calvet, Avignon. Photo: Archives Photographiques

129 Woodcut from Francesco Colonna's *Hypnerotomachia Poliphili* showing the hero in a landscape with classical ruins and armour; Venice (Aldus Manutius), 1499

130 *A Boy Reading*, fresco by Vincenzo Foppa, probably from the destroyed Medici Bank in Milan; the boy may be Giangaleazzo Sforza; *c.* 1455-60. The Wallace Collection, London (Crown Copyright)

131 Drawing of the temple of an ideal city, by Antonio Filarete; *c.* 1460. Biblioteca Nazionale Centrale, Florence

132 Portrait of Francesco Sforza by Francesco Bonsignori; *c.* 1490. National Gallery of Art, Washington, D.C. (Widener Collection)

133 Milan: east end of the cathedral; early 15th C. Photo: Mansell-Alinari

134 Carving of Quintilian by Jörg Syrlin, on the choir stalls of Ulm Cathedral; 1469-74. Photo: Helga Schmidt-Glassner

135 Medal of Guarino da Verona by Matteo de' Pasti; *c.* 1440-46. Courtesy Trustees of the British Museum, London

136 Medal of Vittorino de Feltre by Pisanello; *c.* 1446. British Museum, London. Photo: John Webb (Brompton Studio)

137, 138 Obverse and reverse of medal of Cecilia Gonzaga by Pisanello; 1447. Cecilia had taken the veil in 1444, though this medal shows her in secular dress. Castello Sforzesco, Milan. Photo: Mercantali

139 Opening page from a MS of Lorenzo Valla's *Elegantiae linguae Latinae*, with initial showing the author writing; Italian, mid-15th C. Of all forms of human riches, wrote Valla, nothing excelled the achievement of language, and among ancient languages Latin had special pre-eminence for having spread the fame and rule of Rome in a short space of time throughout the whole of the west: 'for the Roman Empire exists in whatever place the Roman language is ruler'. University Library, Valencia. Photo: Joaquín Adell

140 Oval plaque with portrait of Alberti, thought to be a self-portrait; mid-15th C. Louvre, Paris. Photo: Mansell-Alinari

141 *Trinity with the Virgin, St John, and Donors*, fresco by Masaccio; between 1425 and 1428. Sta Maria Novella, Florence. Photo: Mansell-Alinari

142 Letter X from Luca Pacioli's *De Divina proportione*; Venice, 1509. One of a number of works containing theories of the geometrical construction of the alphabet, of which the earliest was written in the 1460s by Felice

Feliciano of Verona, Pacioli's treatise was completed in 1497 though not published until later.

143 Study in the proportions of the human body, based on Vitruvius, by Leonardo da Vinci; 1492. Accademia, Venice

144 Study for the perspective of an inlaid pavement, by Piero della Francesca, from his *De Prospettiva pingendi*; before 1482. Biblioteca Palatina, Parma. Photo: Todi

145 *The Flagellation* by Piero della Francesca; *c.* 1456. The elaborate geometry of the mosaic pavement is of mystical significance, with Christ standing by a column placed at the centre of a symbolic circle, which is related to other measurements in the painting by intricate calculations. Palazzo Ducale, Urbino. Photo: Mansell-Alinari

146 Rimini: façade of the Tempio Malatestiano, by Alberti; after 1450. Roman in its details and materials (white marble inlaid with coloured marbles and porphyry), it was almost certainly based on a Roman triumphal arch, and has similarities with a surviving Roman city gate at Rimini. Photo: Sadea-Sansoni

147 Reverse of a medal of Sigismondo Malatesta by Matteo de' Pasti, showing the intended elevation of the Tempio Malatestiano at Rimini, with a hemispherical dome; 1450. Matteo de' Pasti was Alberti's engineer on the project. Münzkabinett, Staatliche Museen zu Berlin

148 Florence: dome of the cathedral, by Brunelleschi; begun 1420, finished except for the lantern and some of the stone facing by 1446. A labour force of two to three hundred was used, for whom, when the building was advanced, Brunelleschi devised eating arrangements on the cupola, to prevent wastage of time at midday on the long descent. Photo: Mansell-Alinari

149 *The Trial of St James before Herod*, fresco by Mantegna; completed 1459, destroyed 1944. Eremitani, Padua. Photo: Mansell-Anderson

150 Detail of bronze equestrian statue of Gattamelata by Donatello, commissioned 1443. Piazza del Santo, Padua. Photo: Mansell-Alinari

151 The Abduction of Helen, pen drawing from the *Florentine Picture Chronicle*; by an unknown Florentine artist, *c.* 1460. British Museum, London. Photo: John Freeman

152 *The Miraculous Draught of Fishes*, by Conrad Witz; 1444. Witz's main work was done in Basel, and it must have been as a result of attending the Council of Basel that the bishop of Geneva came to know the painter, and commissioned the altarpiece of which this formed a part. Musée d'Art et d'Histoire, Geneva

153 The Man of Sorrows, woodcut by Dürer from the frontispiece to the *Large Passion*; begun *c.* 1498, published 1511. The presence of the stigmata and the surrounding clouds indicate that this is more than a representation of the mocking of Christ

INDEX   *Numbers in italics refer to illustrations*